NATIONAL
AUDUBON
SOCIETY®

FIRST FIELD GUIDE FISHES

NATIONAL AUDUBON SOCIETY®

FIRST FIELD GUIDE

FISHES

Written by
C. Lavett Smith

Scholastic Inc.
New York Toronto London Auckland Sydney
Mexico City New Delhi Hong Kong

The National Audubon Society, established in 1905, has 550,000 members and more than 500 chapters nationwide. Its mission is to conserve and restore natural ecosystems, focusing on wildlife and plant life, and these guides are part of that mission. Celebrating the beauty and wonders of nature, Audubon looks toward its second century of educating people of all ages. For information about Audubon membership, contact:

National Audubon Society
700 Broadway
New York, NY 10003-9562
800-274-4201
http://www.audubon.org

LIBRARY OF CONGRESS CATALOGING-IN-PUBLICATION DATA

Smith, C. Lavett, 1927–
National Audubon Society first field guide. Fishes / by C. Lavett Smith.
p. cm.
Summary: Explores the world of fishes, discussing their classification, anatomy, behavior, and habitat, and providing photographs and detailed descriptions of individual taxonomic families.
ISBN 0-590-64130-1 (hc). — ISBN 0-590-64198-0 (pbk.)
1. Fishes—Juvenile literature. 2. Fishes—North America—Juvenile literature. [1. Fishes.] I. National Audubon Society.
II. Title. III. Title: First field guide.
QL617.2.S6 1999
597—dc21 99-28106

10 9 8 7 6 5 4 3 2 1 0/0 01 02 03

Printed in Hong Kong 54
First printing, April 2000
Front jacket photograph: Queen Angelfish (*Holacauthus cilirar is*) by Charles V. Angelo/Photo Researchers, Inc.

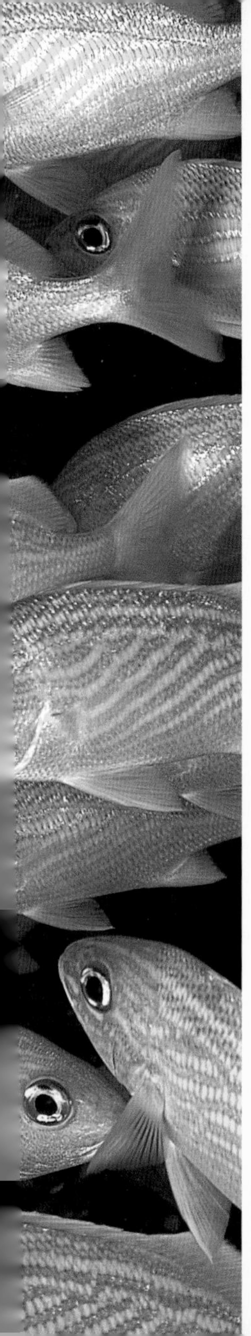

Contents

The world of fishes

How to look at fishes

Field guide

Reference

Scrawled Cowfish page 147

About this book

Whether you see fishes in a lake or stream or during a trip to the seashore, this book will help you learn to look at fishes the way a naturalist does. The book is divided into four parts:

PART 1: The world of fishes gives you lots of interesting information, such as how fishes are named, what makes them perfectly suited to a variety of water habitats, and what these incredibly diverse creatures have in common.

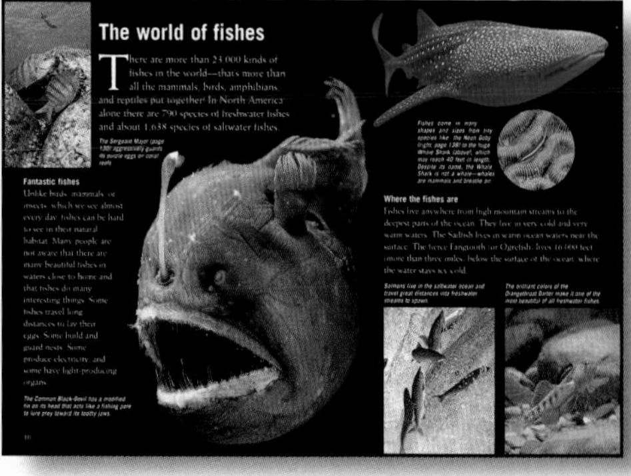

The world of fishes

There are more than 23,000 kinds of fishes in the world—that's more than all the mammals, birds, amphibians, and reptiles put together! In North America alone there are 790 species of freshwater fishes and about 1,638 species of saltwater fishes.

The Sergeant Major (page 130) aggressively guards its purple eggs on coral reefs.

Fantastic fishes

Unlike birds, mammals, or insects, which we see almost every day, fishes can be hard to see in their natural habitat. Many people are not aware that there are many beautiful fishes in waters close to home and that fishes do many interesting things. Some fishes travel long distances to lay their eggs. Some build and guard nests. Some produce electricity, and some have light-producing organs.

The Common Black-Devil has a modified fin on its head that acts like a fishing pole to lure prey toward its toothy jaws.

Fishes come in many shapes and sizes from tiny species like the Neon Goby (right; page 138) to the huge Whale Shark (above), which may reach 40 feet in length. Despite its name, the Whale Shark is not a whale—whales are mammals and breathe air.

Where the fishes are

Fishes live anywhere from high mountain streams to the deepest parts of the ocean. They live in very cold and very warm waters. The Sailfish lives in warm ocean waters near the surface. The fierce Fangtooth (or Ogrefish) lives 16,000 feet (more than three miles) below the surface of the ocean, where the water stays icy cold.

Salmons live in the saltwater ocean and travel great distances into freshwater streams to spawn.

The brilliant colors of the Orangethroat Darter make it one of the most beautiful of all freshwater fishes.

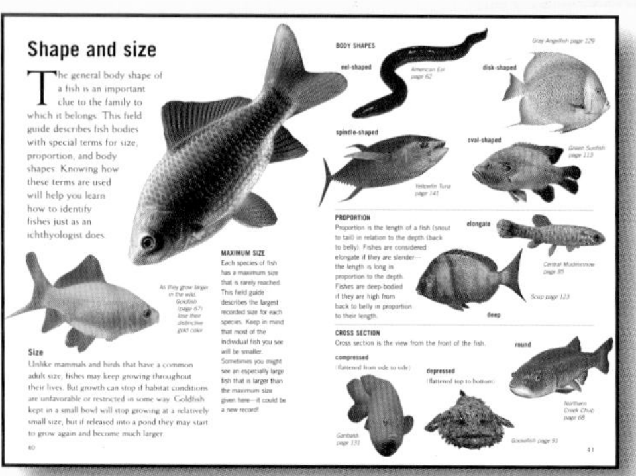

Shape and size

The general body shape of a fish is an important clue to the family to which it belongs. This field guide describes fish bodies with special terms for size, proportion, and body shapes. Knowing how these terms are used will help you learn how to identify fishes just as an ichthyologist does.

As they grow larger in the wild, Goldfish (page 67) lose their distinctive gold color.

Size

Unlike mammals and birds that have a common adult size, fishes may keep growing throughout their lives. But growth can stop if habitat conditions are unfavorable or restricted in some way. Goldfish kept in a small bowl will stop growing at a relatively small size, but if released into a pond they may start to grow again and become much larger.

MAXIMUM SIZE

Each species of fish has a maximum size that is rarely reached. This field guide describes the largest recorded size for each species. Keep in mind that most of the individual fish you see will be smaller. Sometimes you might see an especially large fish that is larger than the maximum size given here—it could be a new record!

40

BODY SHAPES

eel-shaped — *American Eel page 62*

disk-shaped — *Gray Angelfish page 129*

spindle-shaped — *Yellowfin Tuna page 141*

oval-shaped — *Green Sunfish page 113*

PROPORTION

Proportion is the length of a fish (snout to tail) in relation to the depth (back to belly). Fishes are considered elongate if they are slender—the length is long in proportion to the depth. Fishes are deep-bodied if they are high from back to belly in proportion to their length.

elongate — *Central Mudminnow page 85*

deep — *Scup page 123*

CROSS SECTION

Cross section is the view from the front of the fish.

compressed (flattened from side to side) — *Ganbash page 131*

depressed (flattened top to bottom) — *Goosefish page 91*

round — *Northern Creek Chub page 68*

41

PART 2: How to look at fishes tells you what you need to know to begin identifying specific fish—including what they look like; how they eat, swim, and produce young; and where they live.

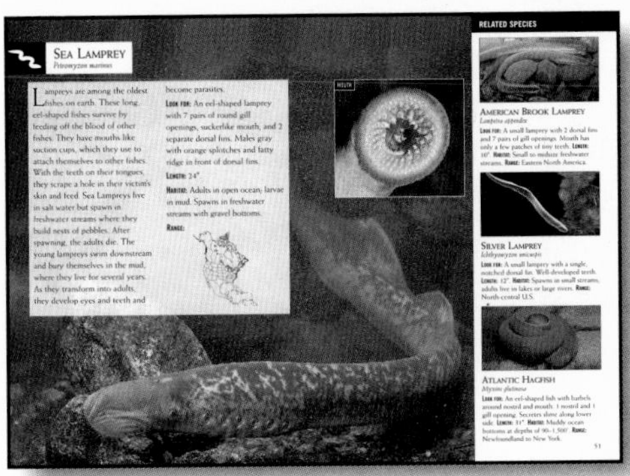

SEA LAMPREY
Petromyzon marinus

Lampreys are among the oldest fishes on earth. These long, eel-shaped fishes survive by feeding off the blood of other fishes. They have mouths like suction cups, which they use to attach themselves to other fishes. With the teeth on their tongues, they scrape a hole in their victim's skin and feed. Sea Lampreys live in salt water but spawn in freshwater streams where they build nests of pebbles. After spawning, the adults die. The young lampreys swim downstream and bury themselves in the mud, where they live for several years. As they transform into adults, they develop eyes and teeth and become parasites.

LOOK FOR: An eel-shaped lamprey with 7 pairs of round gill openings, suckerlike mouth, and 2 separate dorsal fins. Males gray with orange splotches and fatty ridge in front of dorsal fins.

LENGTH: 24".

HABITAT: Adults in open ocean; larvae in mud. Spawns in freshwater streams with gravel bottoms.

RANGE:

MOUTH

RELATED SPECIES

AMERICAN BROOK LAMPREY
Lampetra appendix
LOOK FOR: A small lamprey with 2 dorsal fins and 7 pairs of gill openings. Mouth has only a few patches of tiny teeth. **LENGTH:** 10". **HABITAT:** Small to midsize freshwater streams. **RANGE:** Eastern North America.

SILVER LAMPREY
Ichthyomyzon unicuspis
LOOK FOR: A small lamprey with a single, notched dorsal fin. Well-developed teeth. **LENGTH:** 12". **HABITAT:** Spawns in small streams; adults live in lakes or large rivers. **RANGE:** North-central U.S.

ATLANTIC HAGFISH
Myxine glutinosa
LOOK FOR: An eel-shaped fish with barbels around nostril and mouth. 1 nostril and 1 gill opening. Secretes slime along lower side. **LENGTH:** 31". **HABITAT:** Muddy ocean bottoms at depths of 90–1,500'. **RANGE:** Newfoundland to New York.

51

PART 3: The field guide includes detailed descriptions, range maps, and dramatic photographs of 50 common North American fishes. In addition, this section provides helpful shorter descriptions accompanied by photographs of more than 146 other important species.

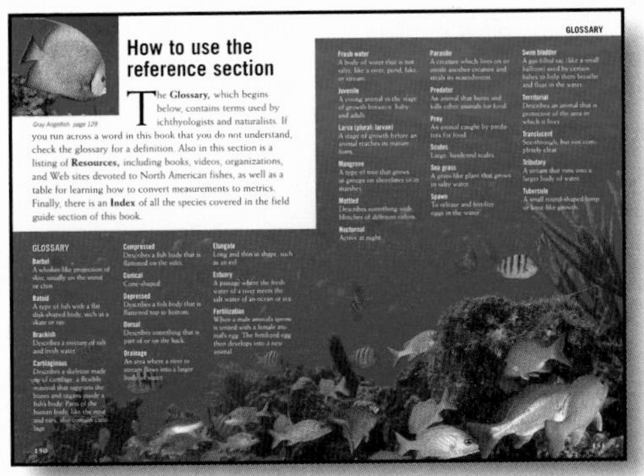

How to use the reference section

Gray Angelfish page 129

The **Glossary,** which begins below, contains terms used by ichthyologists and naturalists. If you run across a word in this book that you do not understand, check the glossary for a definition. Also in this section is a listing of **Resources,** including books, videos, organizations, and Web sites devoted to North American fishes, as well as a table for learning how to convert measurements to metrics. Finally, there is an **Index** of all the species covered in the field guide section of this book.

GLOSSARY

Barbel
A whisker-like projection of skin, usually on the snout or chin.

Batoid
A type of fish with a flat disk-shaped body, such as a skate or ray.

Brackish
Describes a mixture of salt and fresh water.

Cartilaginous
Describes a skeleton made up of cartilage, a flexible material that supports the bones and organs inside a fish's body. Parts of the human body, like the nose and ears, also contain cartilage.

Compressed
Describes a fish body that is flattened on the sides.

Conical
Cone-shaped.

Depressed
Describes a fish body that is flattened top to bottom.

Dorsal
Describes something that is part of or on the back.

Drainage
An area where a river or stream flows into a larger body of water.

Elongate
Long and thin in shape, such as an eel.

Estuary
A passage where the fresh water of a river meets the salt water of an ocean or sea.

Fertilization
When a male animal's sperm is united with a female animal's egg. The fertilized egg then develops into a new animal.

190

GLOSSARY

Fresh water
A body of water that is not salty, like a river, pond, lake, or stream.

Juvenile
A young animal in the stage of growth between baby and adult.

Larva (plural: larvae)
A stage of growth before an animal reaches its mature form.

Mangrove
A type of tree that grows in groups on shorelines or in marshes.

Mottled
Describes something with blotches of different colors.

Nocturnal
Active at night.

Parasite
A creature which lives on or inside another creature and steals its nourishment.

Predator
An animal that hunts and kills other animals for food.

Prey
An animal caught by predators for food.

Scutes
Large, hardened scales.

Sea grass
A grass-like plant that grows in salty water.

Spawn
To release and fertilize eggs in the water.

Swim bladder
A gas-filled sac (like a small balloon) used by certain fishes to help them breathe and float in the water.

Territorial
Describes an animal that is protective of the area in which it lives.

Translucent
See-through, but not completely clear.

Tributary
A stream that runs into a larger body of water.

Tubercule
A small round-shaped lump or knot-like growth.

PART 4: The reference section at the back of the book includes a helpful glossary of terms used by naturalists when they talk about fishes; lists of useful books, Web sites, and organizations; and an index of species covered in the field guide.

What is a naturalist?

A naturalist is a person who studies nature. Some naturalists are scientists, but others are just people who take pleasure in observing animals and plants in the wild. Scientists who study fishes are called ichthyologists (pronounced ick-thee-OLL-oh-jists). You can be a naturalist, too. If you live near a freshwater stream or pond or if you visit the coast, you can begin by looking for fishes from the shore.

A quiet spot by a pond or lake is a great place to start observing fishes.

Charles M. Breder (far right) doing research at the New Jersey shore in the 1920s

FISH-WATCHING SCIENTIST

Charles M. Breder, Jr., (1897–1983) began watching birds near his New Jersey home when he was in high school. He became interested in fishes and spent many hours reading about them at his local public library. Breder spent the rest of his life observing and writing about fish behavior, often combining field observations with carefully controlled experiments in aquariums. Although his formal education ended in high school, he published more than 160 scientific papers and was awarded a college degree in recognition of his scientific observations.

Essential equipment

When you go fish-watching, you will find it helpful to wear sunglasses to reduce glare from the sun reflecting off the water's surface. Binoculars are also useful for observing fishes from the shore. Be sure to carry a notebook and pencils to record what you see and your field guide to help you identify the fishes you spot. Wear footgear you can get wet, such as boots or an old pair of sneakers. Snorkeling is an ideal way to observe fishes if you have been properly instructed and follow all safety rules.

Rules for fish-watching

- Take a friend along with you and make sure to tell an adult where you are going.
- Always wear a life jacket when you are near deep or swift water.
- Respect private property. Ask permission before entering anyone's yard or other property.
- Be careful not to damage stream banks or plants near the shore.
- Whenever possible, do your fish-watching from the shore or from a boat. Try not to disturb the bottom in shallow water and never disturb fish nests.

The world of fishes

There are more than 23,000 kinds of fishes in the world—that's more than all the mammals, birds, amphibians, and reptiles put together! In North America alone there are 790 species of freshwater fishes and about 1,638 species of saltwater fishes.

The Sergeant Major (page 130) aggressively guards its purple eggs on coral reefs.

Fantastic fishes

Unlike birds, mammals, or insects, which we see almost every day, fishes can be hard to see in their natural habitat. Many people are not aware that there are many beautiful fishes in waters close to home and that fishes do many interesting things. Some fishes travel long distances to lay their eggs. Some build and guard nests. Some produce electricity, and some have light-producing organs.

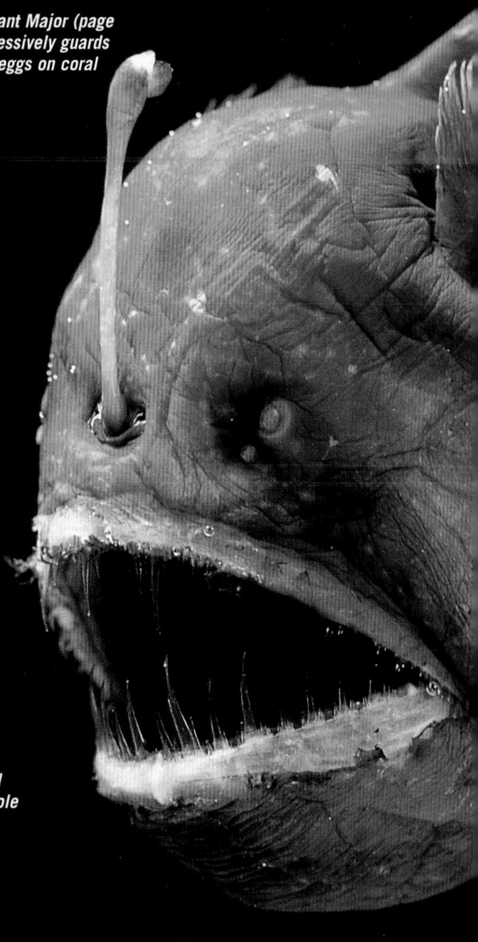

The Common Black-Devil has a modified fin on its head that acts like a fishing pole to lure prey toward its toothy jaws.

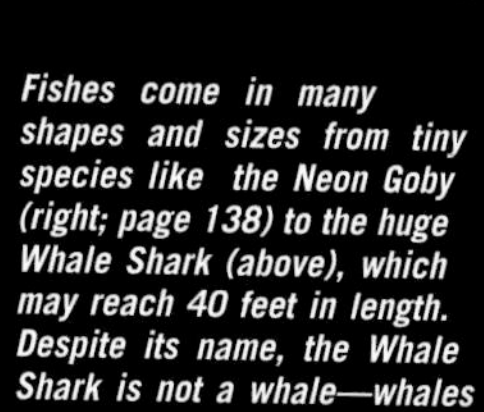

Fishes come in many shapes and sizes from tiny species like the Neon Goby (right; page 138) to the huge Whale Shark (above), which may reach 40 feet in length. Despite its name, the Whale Shark is not a whale—whales are mammals and breathe air.

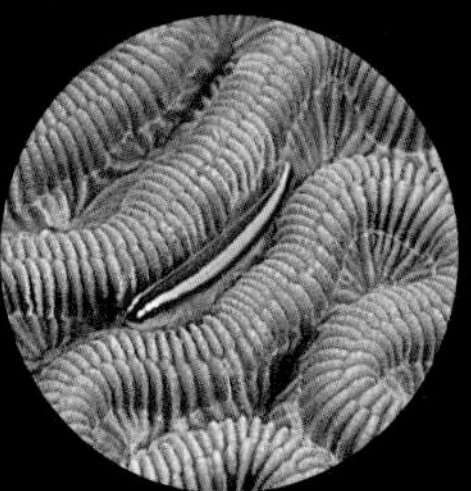

Where the fishes are

Fishes live anywhere from high mountain streams to the deepest parts of the ocean. They live in very cold and very warm waters. The Sailfish lives in warm ocean waters near the surface. The fierce Fangtooth (or Ogrefish) lives 16,000 feet (more than three miles) below the surface of the ocean, where the water stays icy cold.

Salmons live in the saltwater ocean and travel great distances into freshwater streams to spawn.

The brilliant colors of the Orangethroat Darter make it one of the most beautiful of all freshwater fishes.

What's in a name?

Scientists put all animals into groups. The largest group is the animal kingdom and every animal, including fishes, is part of this group. Next, each animal is placed in a group called a phylum. Each phylum is separated into classes, each class into orders, and each order into families. Each family is divided into genera (plural of genus), which are subdivided into species. All fishes are part of the same kingdom and the same phylum.

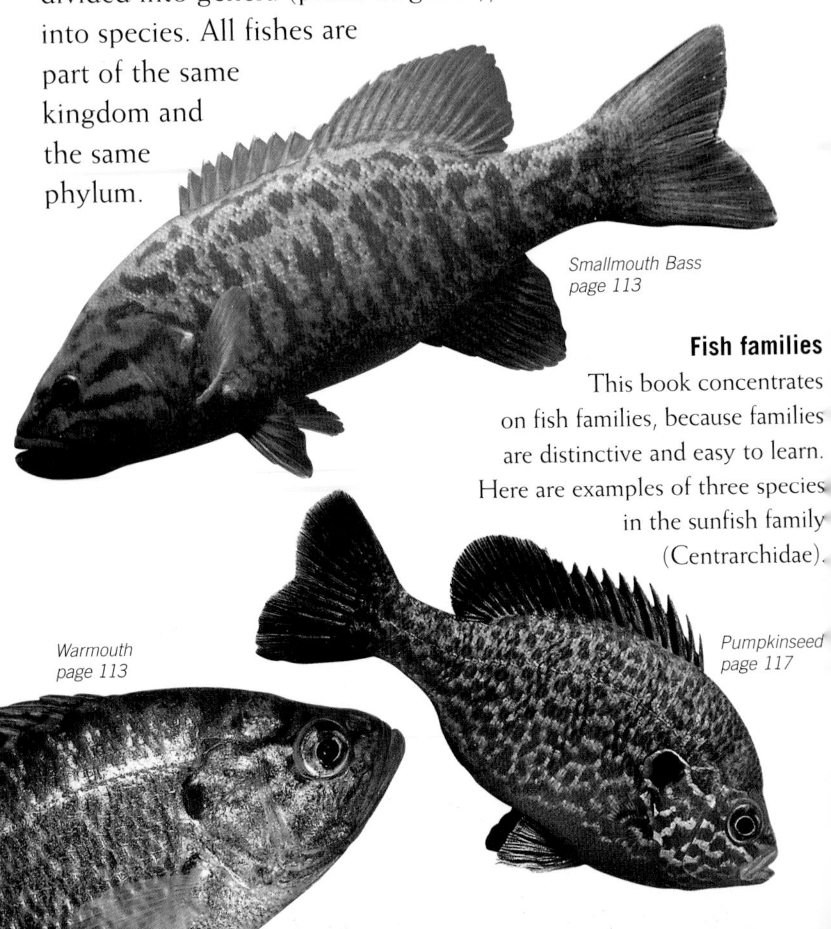

Smallmouth Bass
page 113

Fish families

This book concentrates on fish families, because families are distinctive and easy to learn. Here are examples of three species in the sunfish family (Centrarchidae).

Warmouth
page 113

Pumpkinseed
page 117

Rules of the name game

Most fishes are known by a common name—such as Bluegill—but fishes have other names, too. Scientists give fishes names that are chosen according to a strict set of rules. A scientific name, also called a Latin name, consists of two words: the name of the genus and the name of the species. The scientific name of the Bluegill is *Lepomis macrochirus*. A species has only one scientific name, and this name is recognized all over the world. This guide provides both common and scientific names for specific fishes.

Kingdom: Animalia
Phylum: Chordata
Class: Osteichthyes
Order: Cypriniformes
Family: Cyprinidae
Genus: *Semotilus*
Species: *atromaculatus*
(Creek Chub)

Kingdom: Animalia
Phylum: Chordata
Class: Osteichthyes
Order: Scorpaeniformes
Family: Cottidae
Genus: *Cottus*
Species: *bairdi*
(Mottled Sculpin)

FISH LATIN

As you learn scientific names you will also be learning about history and about the fishes themselves. Sometimes scientific names tell us something about the animal. For example, the species name of the Creek Chub, *atromaculatus,* means "black spot" and refers to the black spot at the base of the dorsal fin. Sometimes a fish is named for a person. The scientific name of the Mottled Sculpin, *Cottus bairdi,* honors S. F. Baird, a 19th-century naturalist and the first U.S. Commissioner of Fisheries.

Fish or fishes?

When we talk about different kinds or species of fish we say "fishes." When we talk about individuals of the same species, we say "fish."

What is a fish?

Fishes are vertebrates, like reptiles, birds, and mammals. This means that they have a spine, or backbone, composed of segments called vertebrae. Fishes come in an amazing variety of shapes and colors, but they all have three important things in common: All fishes live in water, have fins, and use gills to get oxygen from the water.

Lemon Sharks (page 53) are cartilaginous fish

The Lake Sturgeon (page 57) has hard bony scutes along the sides of its body.

SCALES AND SCUTE

Most fishes have scales that cover ar protect their bodies. Scales are made skin and bone. Fishes grow scales ar add new layers throughout their lives. addition to scales, some fishes hav scale-like plates on their bodies calle scutes. This tough stuff forms an extr source of protection from predator The skin of sharks is covered hard, fine scales like small teet Some fishes, like catfishes, hav no scales at all but are covere with tough, flexible ski

The Porkfish (page 124) has many overlapping scales.

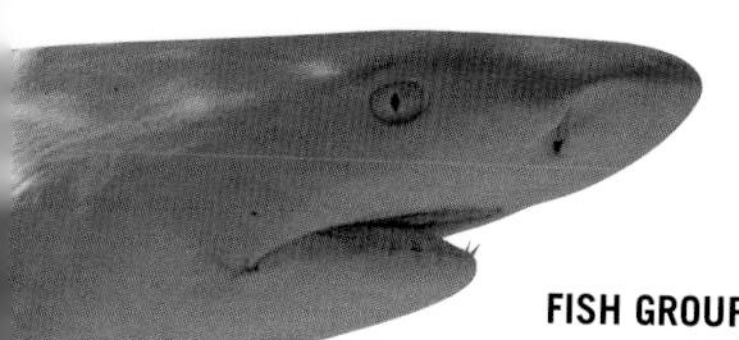

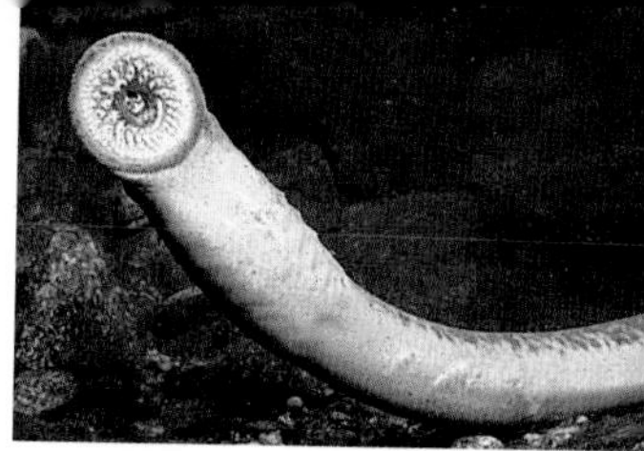

Sea Lampreys (page 50) are jawless fish.

FISH GROUPS

All fishes belong to one of three groups: jawless fishes, cartilaginous fishes, and bony fishes. The jawless fishes include hagfishes and lampreys. They have no jaws and suck in food with their suction-cup-like mouths. Cartilaginous fishes (all sharks and rays) have skeletons made of a flexible but sturdy material called cartilage. Most of the fishes in the world are bony fishes, with skeletons of true bone like other vertebrates. Sunfishes and sea basses are examples of bony fishes.

Smallmouth Basses (page 113) are bony fish.

SLIMY AND COLD-BLOODED

If you've ever held a fish, you know that fish skin feels slimy to the touch. Fishes produce a secretion on their skin that protects them from disease and makes them extra slippery for gliding through the water. Most fishes are cold-blooded (their body is heated by the temperature of the water around them) and some live in icy cold water that is nearly frozen. Fishes have special chemicals in their blood that prevent them from freezing solid.

Scientists took this photograph of a live Coelacanth from inside a deepwater submersible.

FISH FOSSILS

Four hundred million years ago the first fishes swam in the oceans. Scientists today study the fossils of ancient fishes to learn how modern fishes evolved. Some fishes today resemble their ancient ancestors and are called "primitive" fishes. One of the most primitive—and rarest fishes—alive today is the Coelacanth (SEE-la-kanth). Thought to have died out 65 million years ago, this "living fossil" was discovered alive and well in the Indian Ocean in 1938.

Living in water

All animals need oxygen to live. Mammals breathe in (or inhale) air through the mouth and nose and use lungs to get oxygen from the air into their bodies. Fishes "breathe" water and use their gills to extract the oxygen they need.

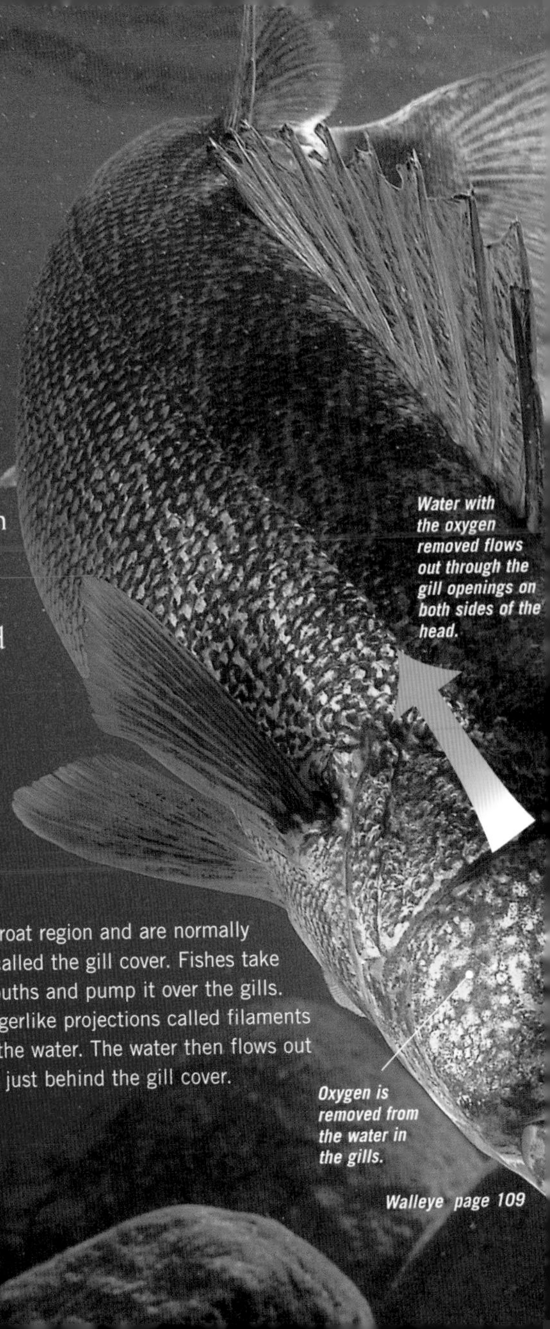

Water with the oxygen removed flows out through the gill openings on both sides of the head.

GILLS

A fish's gills are in the throat region and are normally covered by a bony plate called the gill cover. Fishes take water in through their mouths and pump it over the gills. The gills have rows of fingerlike projections called filaments that absorb oxygen from the water. The water then flows out through the gill openings just behind the gill cover.

Oxygen is removed from the water in the gills.

Walleye page 109

FRESHWATER FISHES

Freshwater fishes absorb water easily and urinate the extra water to stay healthy.

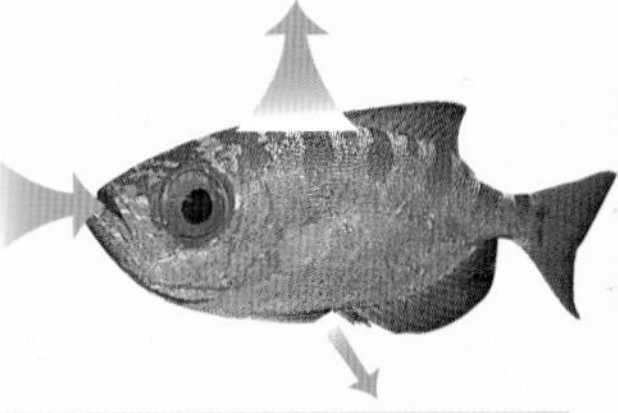

SALTWATER FISHES

Saltwater fishes lose water easily and have to drink constantly to stay healthy.

DO FISHES DRINK?

Although fishes live in water, they still have to keep the proper balance of water inside their bodies. Saltwater fishes lose water through their skin and must drink salty water to stay alive. They also have to get rid of the extra salt. How do they do it? They have special cells in their gills that remove salt from the blood. Freshwater fishes have the opposite problem. Water tends to move into their bodies rather than out. They have to get rid of this extra water by expelling large amounts of urine.

GULPERS

A few fishes have the ability to get oxygen from air as well as from water. One of these special fishes is the Alligator Gar. If there is not enough oxygen in the water where it lives, it gulps air at the surface. It then uses its specialized swim bladder to absorb the extra oxygen it needs.

Oxygen-rich water enters the mouth and is pumped over the gills.

Alligator Gars page 59

Great Barracudas (left; page 141) swim with amazing bursts of speed, slicing through the water to catch and eat their favorite foods: fast-moving smaller fishes and speedy squids.

Locomotion

Locomotion means how something moves from place to place through a medium like air or water. Water is about 50 times as thick as air, so most fishes are streamlined to slip easily through their watery habitats: Their heads are connected directly to their bodies without a neck, and their fins are close in to their bodies.

The Manta (right; page 55) and other skates and rays are flattened and disk-shaped. They move through the water by flapping their wing fins. Remora fish often attach themselves to Mantas and ride along.

SWIM BLADDERS

All fishes have an organ called a swim bladder that is filled with gas. By adding or subtracting the amount of gas (mostly oxygen) in the swim bladder, fishes control how much they float in the water. Without a swim bladder, fishes would have to swim constantly to hold a position at any depth beneath the water.

The Walking Catfish (below) actually walks across land to move from one body of water to another. It uses its pectoral fins like legs and has a modified gill chamber to get oxygen from the air.

Billfishes like the Sailfish (page 140) are some of the fastest fishes in the sea. They can swim for short periods at over 70 miles per hour!

SWIM LIKE A FISH

Most fishes propel themselves through the water by moving their bodies in S-shaped waves. Below are examples of typical fish shapes (shown from above) and the way fishes with these shapes swim.

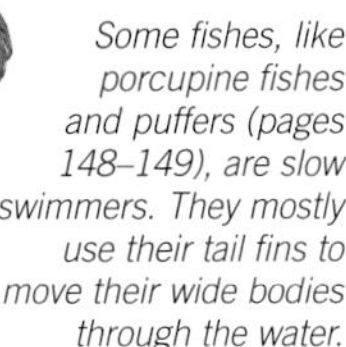

Some fishes, like porcupine fishes and puffers (pages 148–149), are slow swimmers. They mostly use their tail fins to move their wide bodies through the water.

Eels and lampreys slither, similar to snakes on land, pushing their heads forward and moving their slender bodies in a series of waves.

Catfishes and jacks have broad heads and bodies. They use less of the whole body to swim than eels do.

Salmons and minnows move with the powerful back half of the body and use their large tails to push themselves along.

Sharks and tunas use the rear third of the body and have strong muscles in their tails that make them very speedy.

FISH SCHOOL

Some fish of the same species live in large groups called schools. They band together to protect themselves from predators, to migrate, and to search for food. Fish schools can contain thousands of individuals.

A school of Gray Snappers (page 120)

Senses

Fishes have the same five senses that humans have: sight, hearing, touch, smell, and taste. They use their senses to look for food, avoid predators, find a partner to spawn with, and to find their way around their habitat. Many fishes have highly adapted senses that allow them to smell food from very far away or detect vibrations in the water.

FISH EYES

Fishes' eyes ar like humans' eyes but they focus in a different way. Humans have muscles that change the shape o the lens in the eye, bu fishes have muscles that move their lenses back and forth. They focus on objects much as a camera focuses. Fishes see in color, just as people do.

FISH EARS

Although fishes have no external ears (their ears are inside their head), they still have a keen sense of hearing. Some fishes communicate by making sounds and listening for a response from a member of their own species.

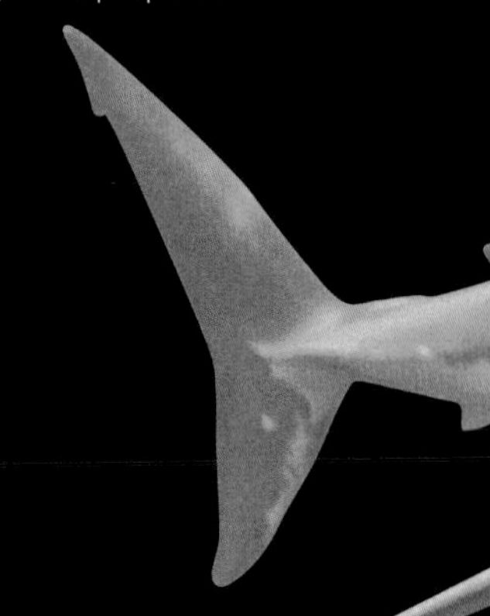

The Brown Bullhead (page 78) uses its barbels (or whiskers) to find food in murky waters and to find other catfishes.

FISHY TASTE

Human tastebuds are on the tongue but in some fishes the tastebuds are scattered over the outside of the body! The tastebuds of catfishes are concentrated on barbels, the whiskerlike projections near the mouth.

LATERAL LINE

Fishes have a special sense organ called the lateral line that detects vibrations in the water. It runs along both sides of the fish just below the skin and sometimes appears as a thin black stripe. Fishes use the lateral line to sense movement in the water, the temperature of the water, and to maintain their balance.

Scup page 123

DO FISHES SMELL?

The smell detectors in fishes are in sacs in front of the eyes. Fishes smell by pumping water in through two front nostrils and use these smell detectors to sample chemicals in the water. The water then passes out through the rear two nostrils.

White Shark page 53

Sharks have an amazing sense of smell. Even under the sea they can detect very small amounts of blood and oil from an injured fish miles away.

ELECTRIC FISHES

Some fishes can detect weak electrical currents in the water using special organs called electroreceptors. They use this ability mostly to "sense" when other fishes are nearby. Other fishes, like electric rays and catfishes, produce a powerful electrical charge that stuns their prey.

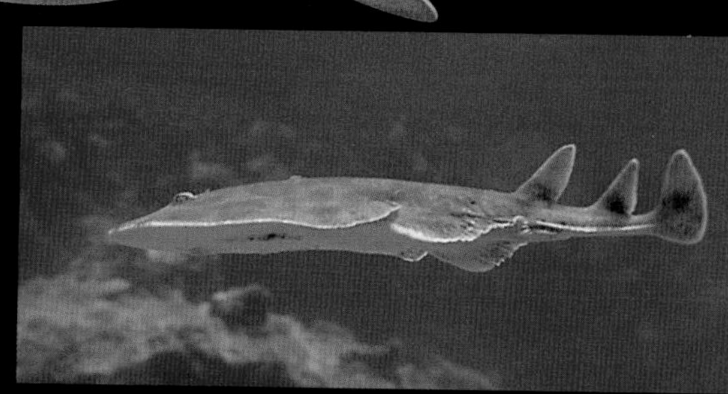

The Lesser Electric Ray (page 55) delivers an electric shock to stun its prey.

What do fishes eat?

Fishes eat many kinds of food, including insects, worms, snails, clams, and other fishes. Only a few kinds of fishes eat plants. Fishes will usually eat whatever is plentiful and easy to catch, but most are specialized in some way to feed on a particular food. You can get an idea of what a fish likes to eat by studying its teeth and the shape of its body.

THROAT TEETH

Besides the teeth that grow out of their jaws, some fishes also have teeth located behind the gills near the throat. They use them to eat prey in much the same way as they would use their regular teeth. Minnows and suckers have no teeth in their mouths. They shred, crush, and chew up all their food using their throat teeth.

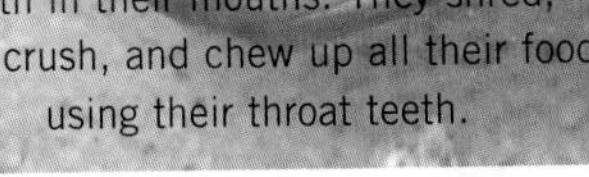

CHASERS AND POUNCERS

How a fish catches its prey depends on the shape of its body. Slender, streamlined species, like billfishes, are fast swimmers that chase down speedy prey over a distance. Fishes with stout bodies, like basses, lie in wait for prey and ambush it when it swims by. Sunfishes have short, compressed bodies that enable them to make quick sharp turns and chase prey through vegetation.

The heavy-bodied Largemouth Bass (page 112) is built for speed over a short distance.

RAKING IT IN

Some fishes feed mainly on plankton (small plants and animals that drift freely in the open water). They use bony parts in the mouth and throat called gill rakers to strain prey out of water passing through the gills.

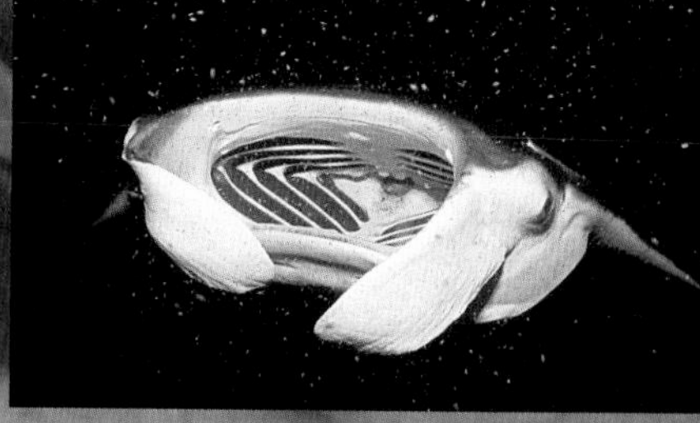

The Manta (page 55) swims with its mouth open to strain food from the water.

CHEW ON THIS

Fishes usually swallow their food whole, but some have special teeth for shredding food or for crushing shells. Fishes like gars and pikes use their sharp, pointed teeth to grab and hold their prey before swallowing. Damselfishes and other species with patches of short, blunt teeth eat mostly small, soft-shelled animals. The Freshwater Drum crushes clams, snails, and other hard-shelled animals with its large throat teeth before it swallows them.

The Stoplight Parrotfish (page 135) uses its beaklike teeth to munch on plants and creatures like sea anemones on coral reefs.

VEGETARIAN MENU

Only a few fishes feed on plants, but those that do have specially designed teeth and intestines to help them digest vegetation. Teeth with flat surfaces are used for grinding plants. Very long intestines allow digestive fluids more time to work on the food.

The Grass Carp (page 67) eats large amounts of vegetation in freshwater streams and lakes.

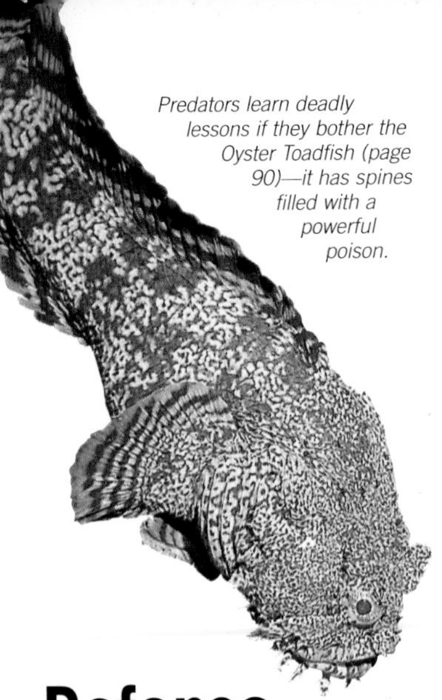

Predators learn deadly lessons if they bother the Oyster Toadfish (page 90)—it has spines filled with a powerful poison.

Defense

Like most animals, fishes have to find food to eat and at the same time avoid being eaten by other animals. Fishes defend themselves in many ways, including swimming away from predators or blending into the background. Some puff up their bodies so they can't be swallowed. Many fishes are also protected by pointy spines and hard, scaly skin.

CAMOUFLAGE COLOR

One way fishes hide from their enemies is by camouflage (blending into the background of their habitat). Sometimes a fish can remain perfectly still, and if it is the right color and shape, its predator may not see it, even when they are looking right at it. Camouflage also works the other way: It makes a predator hard to see as it stalks its prey.

Winter Flounder (page 145) live on the bottom in saltwater bays and oceans, blending into the soft mud and sand. Bigger fishes swim by and don't notice them at all.

Sargassumfish (page 91) are colored to match the seaweed that floats where they live. It protects them from hungry predators, but it also makes them nearly invisible to prey.

Muskellunge (page 85) are big fish with enormous appetites. They hide quietly in grassy areas of fresh water, ready to attack and eat fishes and frogs that swim by.

'OINTY SPINES

Лany fishes have ·pines to protect hem from their :nemies. Spines are ·harp bones usually ɔcated near the ins or on the head. ;ome species have ·pines that are flat ·gainst the body ınd can be pointed ›utward to discourage ›redators.

Vhen threatened by a predator, the 'orcupinefish (page 149) fills itself ʻith water and puffs up like a spiky ball. 'he predator usually swims away, 'iscouraged and hungry.

ODY ARMOR

Longnose Gar (page 58)

·cales are a kind f armor. Some fishes ave extremely hard, bony :ales that provide excellent protection. he Longnose Gar has tough diamond-shaped scales 'l over its body that protect it from predators.

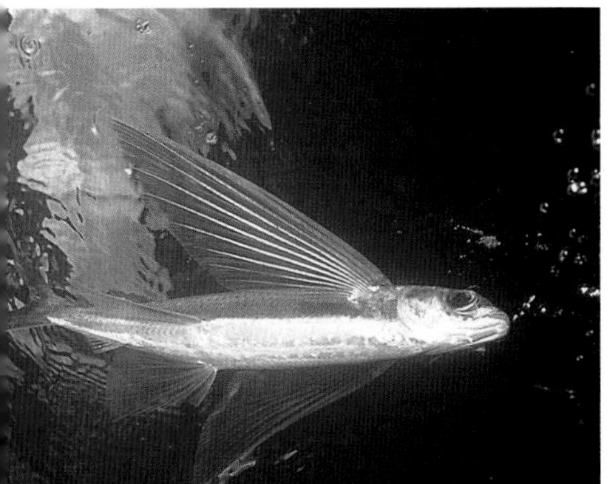

ESCAPE

When approached by a predator or some other threat, the first reaction of most fishes is to swim away. Some try to escape into open water; others swim to shelter among weeds, or around submerged rocks or logs.

Escaping hungry predators, the Atlantic Flyingfish (right; page 94) swims swiftly along the surface of the water and takes off into the air for short periods.

Nesting and reproduction

Sockeye Salmon in spawning colors

Most fishes reproduce by external fertilization—a female fish releases eggs into the water, where they are fertilized by sperm from a male. This process is called spawning. Some fishes, such as sharks, reproduce by internal fertilization—the male deposits sperm into the female fish, where the eggs are fertilized. These fishes are called "livebearers," which means that they give birth to live young.

Trout eggs hatching

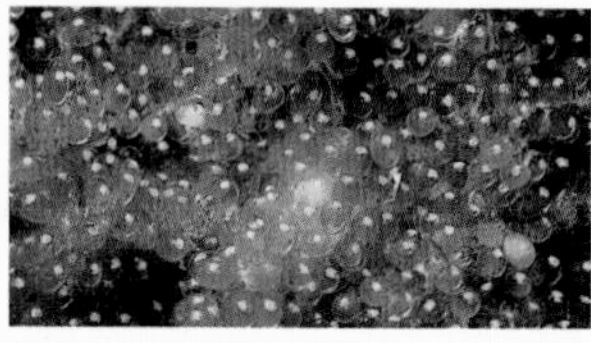

A mass of Garibaldi (page 131) eggs

FISH EGGS

Fish eggs range in size from a barely visible dot to the size of a pea. Some eggs float in the open water, while others are heavier than water and sink to the bottom. Eggs on the bottom may clump together in masses, or they may stick to sand grains or to hard objects. Some fishes carefully place eggs on the undersides of rocks or on sticks in the water. Some eggs are not sticky at all and simply fall into the spaces between pebbles. Fish eggs may hatch within several days of spawning or many weeks later, depending on the species and the water temperature.

SPAWNING RUN

Many fishes move to special areas where conditions are just right for spawning and protecting their eggs. For some minnows and sunfishes, this is a matter of moving a few yards in a stream or into shallow water in a lake. But for salmons and shads, it can mean a journey of thousands of miles.

Gizzard Shad page 63

Fish attraction

Many fishes develop bright colors during their breeding seasons. Usually it is the male that is more colorful. He uses his bright colors to attract females. Color also makes it easier for fishes to recognize members of their own species.

A male Bluegill (page 116) in breeding colors

SALMON LIFE CYCLE

Coho Salmon spend part of their lives in the salt water of the Pacific Ocean, but they travel many miles into freshwater streams and rivers to spawn. Along the journey, their bodies change to a brilliant red color. Females release eggs along the gravel bottom, where they are fertilized by males. Both males and females die after spawning. The young fish hatch and spend a year in the fresh water before traveling out to sea. Two to three years later, the salmon return to the river as breeding adults. They spawn, and the cycle continues.

Coho Salmon (page 83) gather in streams to spawn.

Fish nests

Many fishes simply release their eggs and sperm into the water and pay no attention at all to the fertilized eggs, but other fishes build nests and guard the eggs and young. Fishes usually spawn during a particular time of year. In freshwater ponds and lakes, late spring and early summer are excellent times to observe fishes making nests and laying eggs. It's also a good time to observe hatchlings (baby fishes) schooling together.

The male Yellowhead Jawfish protects the fertilized eggs by keeping them in his mouth until they hatch.

The male Redbreast Sunfish guards its nest to keep hungry predators away.

The Striped Shiner (page 70) spawns and smaller fishes will raid the nest to eat the eggs. Some eggs survive to mature into hatchlings.

FISH PARENTING

Most fish parents spend little time caring for their offspring. But some, such as certain catfishes, guard the nests and young for a few days after the eggs hatch. In a few species the adults carry eggs on their bodies. Some fishes actually keep the eggs in their mouths until they hatch.

Baby fishes

When young fishes hatch they may look very different from adult fish of their species. Newly hatched fishes may be nearly transparent, but in a few days they develop color patterns. Juvenile freshwater fishes tend to resemble their parents, but most saltwater fishes have larval stages. These larval fish drift freely in the open sea; many are bizarre-looking, with odd shapes or long trailing fins.

Newly hatched salmon (called sacfry) look very different from their parents.

Juvenile trout (called fry) look like miniature versions of the adult form.

The juvenile Goosefish (page 91) has wide, sail-like fins it loses as it matures.

The male Garibaldi (page 131) guards its nest for two to three weeks until the eggs hatch.

Where do fishes live?

Field guides like this one tell you two things about where a fish lives: its range and its habitat. The range is the geographic area where the fish lives, such as the Great Lakes or the Atlantic Ocean. The habitat is the type of aquatic environment where a species of fish lives. Temperature, amount of salt and oxygen in the water, and water movement are the key factors that define which fishes can live in a particular place. Although each kind of fish is adapted to live in a special environment, almost every kind of watery habitat is home to some fish species. Learning about where fishes live is important for fish-watching and identification.

OCEANS

The oceans of the world cover 70 percent of the earth's surface and are home to most species of fishes. Oceans vary in temperature and oxygen content, but they all have one thing in common: salt. Some fishes live miles under the surface in the coldest watery depths of the ocean, while others spend their lives in the warmer water near the surface. Still other fishes live part of the time in open ocean (water far from land) and travel to water closer to the land to feed and spawn. Examples of open ocean fishes are the Sailfish, Sea Lamprey, Sargassumfish, and Yellowfin Tuna (pictured; page 141).

COASTAL WATERS

Coastal ocean habitats include all salt water close to land. The water is usually shallower than in open ocean habitats. The Nurse Shark, Atlantic Stingray, Striped Bass (pictured; page 104), California Grunion, and Lined Seahorse live in coastal ocean habitats.

CORAL REEFS

Coral reefs are warm-water coastal habitats. Home to the greatest variety of fishes anywhere, reefs have everything a fish could want: lots of oxygen in the water, fairly low salt levels, plenty of shelter on the reef, and an abundant food supply. The Goldspotted Snake Eel, Squirrelfish, Trumpetfish, and Queen Angelfish (pictured; page 129) are all coral reef fishes.

ESTUARIES

Estuaries, bays, and salt marshes are habitats where fresh water from land meets salt water from oceans. These waters are less salty than the open ocean and contain a rich variety of food and shelter for fishes. Many fishes move into estuaries to spawn. The Winter Flounder (pictured; page 145), Atlantic Sturgeon, White Perch, Striped Bass, and American Eel all find a home in estuaries.

PONDS AND LAKES

Ponds and lakes form wherever fresh water is stopped from flowing freely. The main difference between ponds and lakes is size and depth, but they share many of the same species. Ponds and lakes have a variety of different habitats where certain

STREAMS AND RIVERS

Freshwater streams and rivers are habitats with flowing fresh water. They have many types of habitats where particular fish live. The water can be very fast- or slow-moving, and the temperature can range from icy cold to bathtub warm. The Brook Trout (pictured; page 80) and Grayling live in fast-moving cold-water streams and rivers. The Common Carp and Paddlefish live in warmer, slower-flowing rivers.

fish may be found. The Blacknose Dace (pictured left; page 73), Grass Pickerel, and Pumpkinseed live in vegetation close to shore. The White Bass (pictured right; page 105) and Walleye are usually found in deeper parts of lakes.

Range

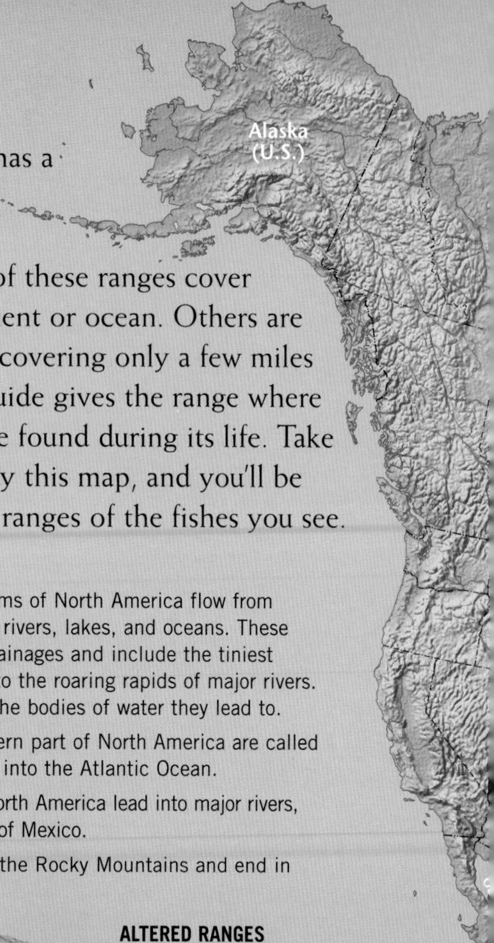

Each fish species has a natural range, where it spends most of its life. Some of these ranges cover a large part of a continent or ocean. Others are very small, sometimes covering only a few miles of stream. This field guide gives the range where a particular fish may be found during its life. Take a few moments to study this map, and you'll be prepared to locate the ranges of the fishes you see.

Alaska (U.S.)

STREAM DRAINAGES

The freshwater rivers and streams of North America flow from mountains and drain into large rivers, lakes, and oceans. These waterways are called stream drainages and include the tiniest trickle of creeks in mountains to the roaring rapids of major rivers. All drainages are named after the bodies of water they lead to.

- Stream drainages of the eastern part of North America are called Atlantic drainages. They lead into the Atlantic Ocean.
- Stream drainages of central North America lead into major rivers, the Great Lakes, and the Gulf of Mexico.
- Pacific drainages are west of the Rocky Mountains and end in the Pacific Ocean.

The Brown Trout (page 81) is not native to North America. Originally from Europe, it was widely introduced by anglers for sport in the 19th century.

ALTERED RANGES

The natural ranges of many fishes have been altered by human interference. Sometimes fishes were purposely moved into certain areas in order to improve fishing for food or sport. Sometimes fishes were introduced accidentally as anglers discarded live bait or ships pumped out ballast water (water used for balance in the hulls of boats) that contained fishes.

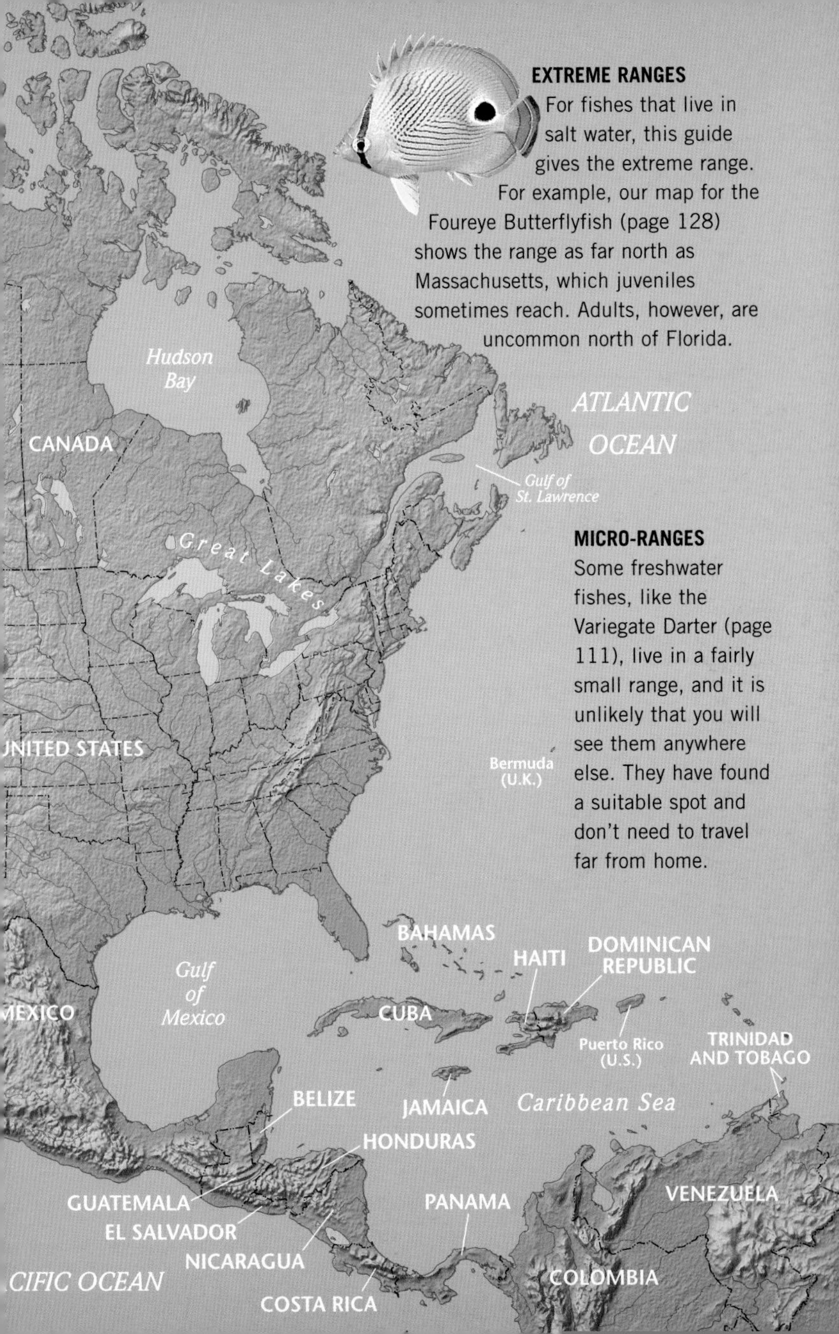

EXTREME RANGES

For fishes that live in salt water, this guide gives the extreme range. For example, our map for the Foureye Butterflyfish (page 128) shows the range as far north as Massachusetts, which juveniles sometimes reach. Adults, however, are uncommon north of Florida.

MICRO-RANGES

Some freshwater fishes, like the Variegate Darter (page 111), live in a fairly small range, and it is unlikely that you will see them anywhere else. They have found a suitable spot and don't need to travel far from home.

How to see fishes

Although many fishes live in deep water and never come close to the surface, others spend all or part of their lives in water that is shallow enough that they can be seen from the shore. It takes patience and sometimes luck to see fishes, but it is always worth looking down into the water whenever you get the chance.

Small ponds in spring and summer are excellent places for fish-watching.

SHADY SPOT

Sunglasses help to cut surface glare so that you can see into the water. On a sunny day, position yourself with the sun your back instead of in your face. This wi help cut down on surface glare so you ca see the fishes below.

APPROACH IS EVERYTHING

Approach shorelines slowly and quietly. Fishes can see out of the water quite well and can spot you better than you think. Your shadow might even frighten them away.

Fishes are always on the lookout for hungry predators, such as Ospreys, that would like to eat them.

you have a chance to use a mask and snorkel, you can see fishes underwater, too.

IGHT FISHING

ishes are very active at night, and many come into shallow water. With an adult, go o the shore of a small pond or lake and shine your flashlight into the water. You may ee minnows and other fishes schooling around the light.

NGLING

nother way to see fishes is to atch them on a hook and line or o find an angler who has caught a ish and is willing to show it to you. entle release the fish you catch, nless you plan to eat them, and bey local rules for when and here you are allowed to fish.

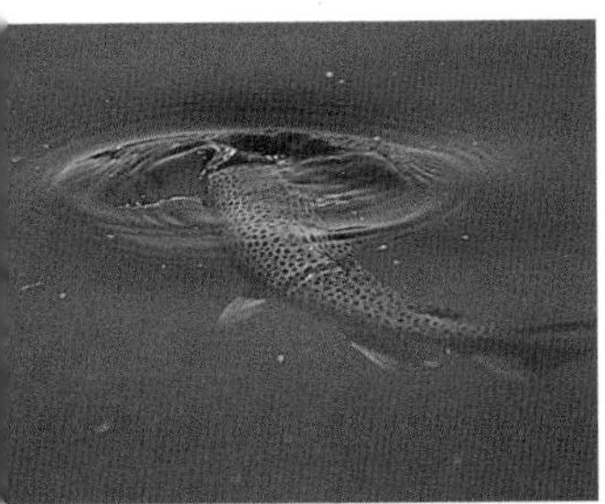

FISH RISING

Another good way to observe fishes is to watch the water surface. Many fishes feed on insects, frogs, or small fishes as they float near the surface. When a fish comes from below to gulp prey into its mouth, you can see a circle, called a rise, form on the surface. Sometimes fishes swim so fast to catch prey that they jump completely out of the water.

How to identify fishes

This field guide is designed to introduce you to the fishes that live in the fresh and salt waters of North America. Because there are nearly 2,500 species in the region, it is not possible to describe them all here. It is more important to recognize the common families in our region and to get some idea of how fishes are related. You will learn how sharks, skates, and rays are similar, that minnows, suckers, and catfishes are closely related, and that perches, sea basses, and sunfishes have many features in common.

The Hogfish (page 133) has three very long spines on its first dorsal fin.

APPEARANCE

The first step in identifying any fish is to look at its overall appearance. This includes shape, color, and special features such as fin spines and barbels.

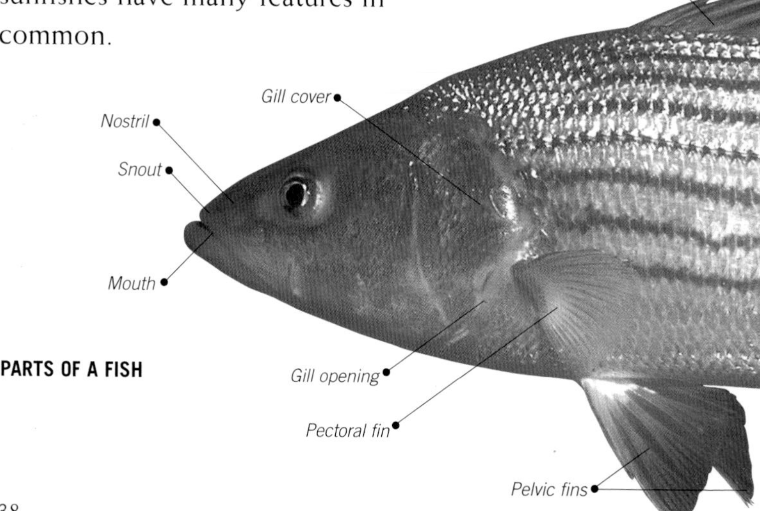

PARTS OF A FISH

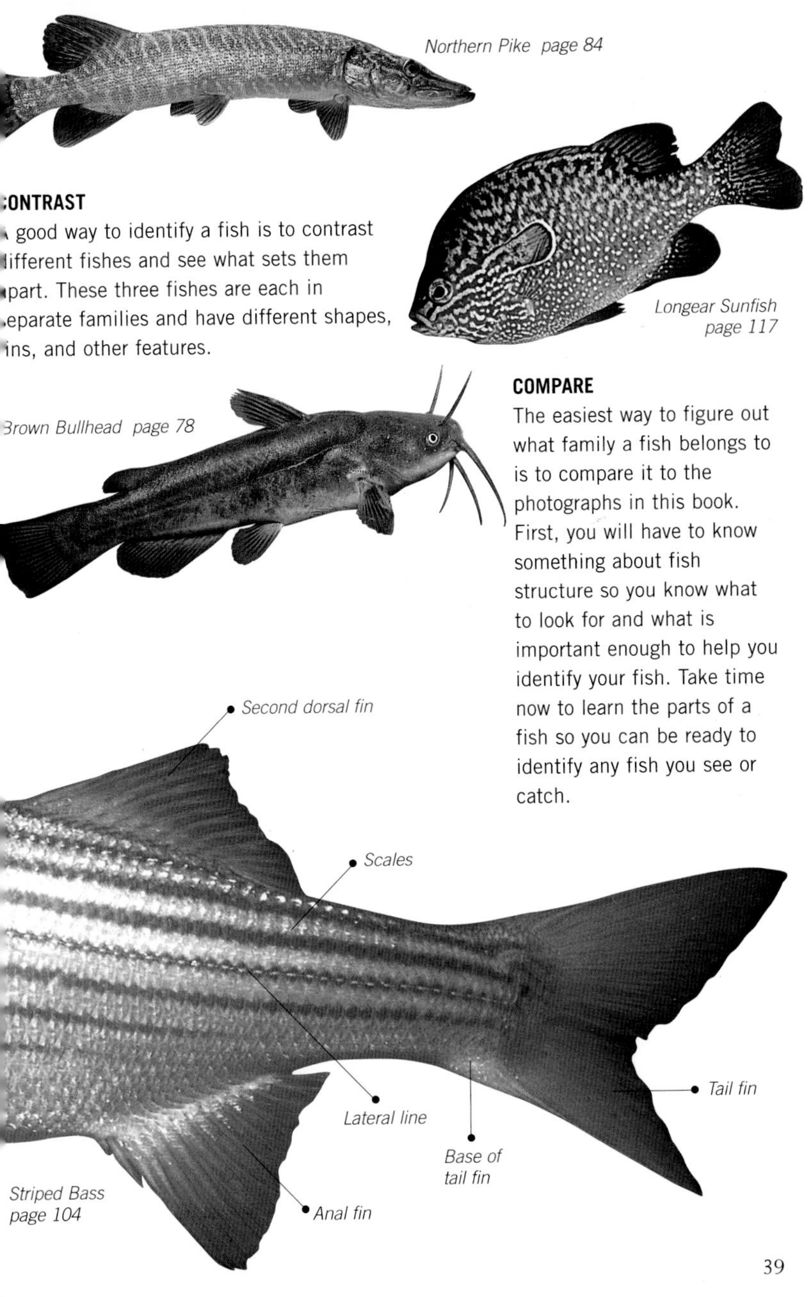

Northern Pike page 84

Longear Sunfish page 117

Brown Bullhead page 78

Striped Bass page 104

CONTRAST

A good way to identify a fish is to contrast different fishes and see what sets them apart. These three fishes are each in separate families and have different shapes, fins, and other features.

COMPARE

The easiest way to figure out what family a fish belongs to is to compare it to the photographs in this book. First, you will have to know something about fish structure so you know what to look for and what is important enough to help you identify your fish. Take time now to learn the parts of a fish so you can be ready to identify any fish you see or catch.

Shape and size

The general body shape of a fish is an important clue to the family to which it belongs. This field guide describes fish bodies with special terms for size, proportion, and body shapes. Knowing how these terms are used will help you learn how to identify fishes just as an ichthyologist does.

As they grow larger in the wild, Goldfish (page 67) lose their distinctive gold color.

Size

Unlike mammals and birds that have a common adult size, fishes may keep growing throughout their lives. But growth can stop if habitat conditions are unfavorable or restricted in some way. Goldfish kept in a small bowl will stop growing at a relatively small size, but if released into a pond they may start to grow again and become much larger.

MAXIMUM SIZE

Each species of fish has a maximum size that is rarely reached. This field guide describes the largest recorded size for each species. Keep in mind that most of the individual fish you see will be smaller. Sometimes you might see an especially large fish that is larger than the maximum size given here—it could be a new record!

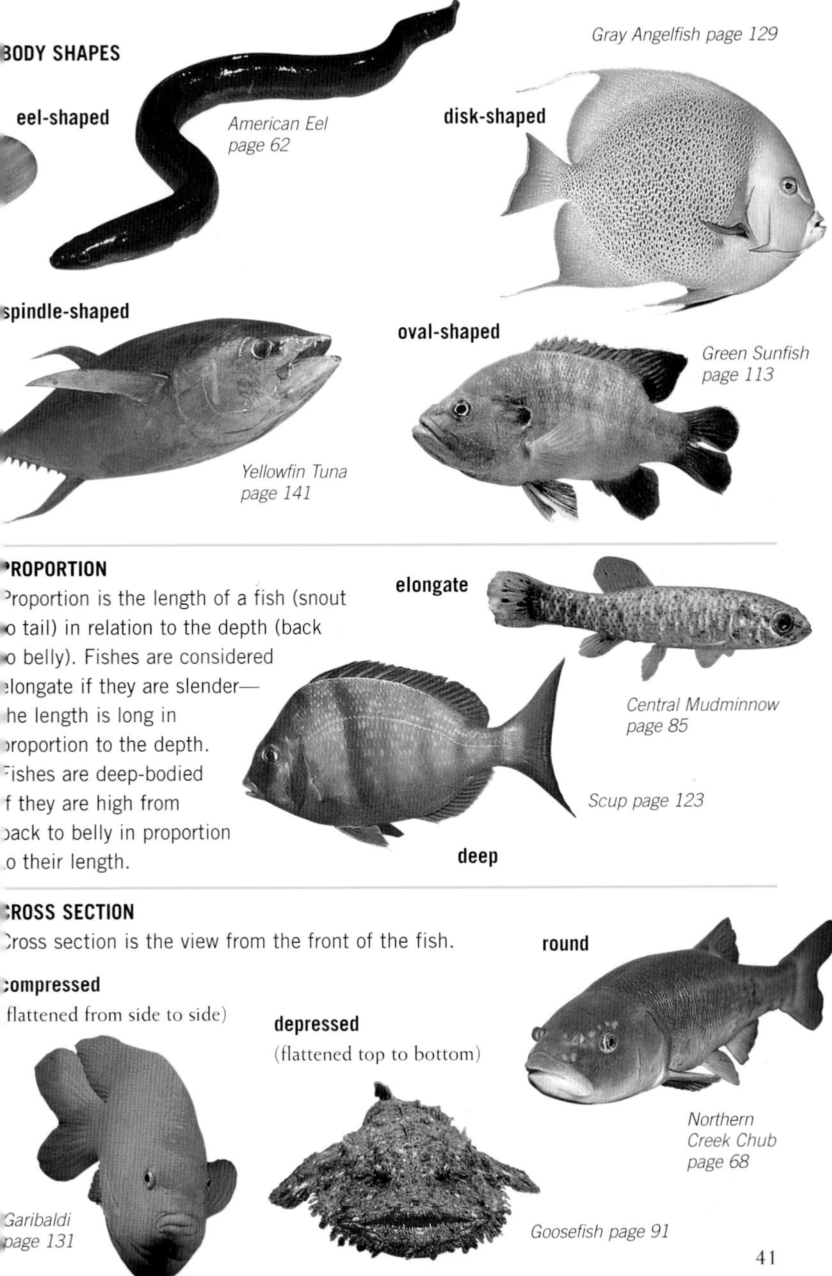

BODY SHAPES

eel-shaped

American Eel page 62

disk-shaped

Gray Angelfish page 129

spindle-shaped

Yellowfin Tuna page 141

oval-shaped

Green Sunfish page 113

PROPORTION

Proportion is the length of a fish (snout to tail) in relation to the depth (back to belly). Fishes are considered elongate if they are slender—the length is long in proportion to the depth. Fishes are deep-bodied if they are high from back to belly in proportion to their length.

elongate

Central Mudminnow page 85

deep

Scup page 123

CROSS SECTION

Cross section is the view from the front of the fish.

compressed
(flattened from side to side)

Garibaldi page 131

depressed
(flattened top to bottom)

Goosefish page 91

round

Northern Creek Chub page 68

Fins

All fishes have fins, and fins come in many shapes and sizes. Some fishes have short, stubby fins, while others have long, flowing fins. The important thing to remember is that most closely related fishes have similar fins. Counting a fin's spines and rays can really help with fish identification. It can be tricky, but spend some time learning about fins, and you'll master an important step in identifying fishes.

The Gray Angelfish (page 129) has long, flowing fins.

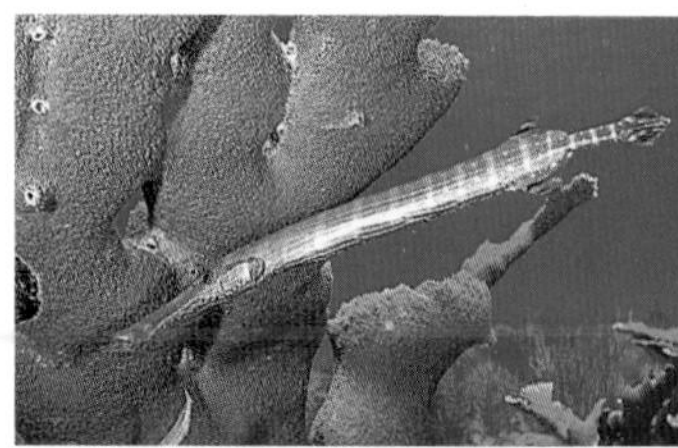

The Trumpetfish (page 103) has short, stubby fins.

FIN RAYS

Fins are made of layers of skin supported by bony rods called fin rays. There are two kinds of fin rays: soft rays and spiny rays. Spiny rays are simply called spines.

SOFT RAYS

Soft rays bend and are usually divided into smaller branches toward the edge of the fin.

The Brook Stickleback (page 100) has five dorsal spines.

SPINE COUNTING

Sometimes closely related fishes differ in having more or fewer rays (soft rays and spines) in the fins. The Threespine Stickleback has three dorsal spines and the Fourspine Stickleback has—you guessed it—four dorsal spines.

ADIPOSE FIN

A few fishes have a fin near the base of the tail called an adipose fin.

Grayling page 83

DORSAL FINS

Some fishes have a single dorsal fin, which may be short or long. Others have two or even three dorsal fins. Sometimes the dorsal fin consists of spines in front and soft rays in back. These sections can be continuous (all together), notched, or divided into separate fins, either close together or far apart.

The Yellow Perch (page 108) has two dorsal fins.

TAIL FINS

Tail fin shapes are also useful for identifying fishes. Tails can be forked, squarish, rounded, or in some cases—like the eels and rays—they can be pointed. Forked tails can be deeply forked or shallowly forked or somewhere in-between.

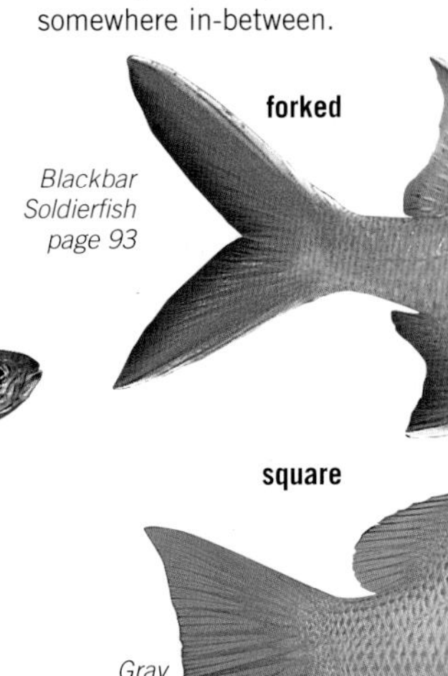

forked

Blackbar Soldierfish page 93

square

Gray Snapper page 120

rounded

Brook Stickleback page 100

pointed

Goldspotted Snake Eel page 63

Colors and patterns

Fishes tend to blend in with the environment in which they live. Some fishes, especially those that live in warm seas with colorful underwater plants and creatures, are as brightly colored as flowers. Those that live in lakes and ponds are usually less colorful. The patterns on a fish are important too. Stripes and spots can provide helpful clues to a fish's identification.

Colors of the rainbow

Color is one of the first things you will notice about fishes and one of the most important ways to recognize and identify them. Native fishes of North America come in a wide array of colors, including yellow, red, black, blue, brown, olive, bronze, silver, and white. Many ocean fishes are silvery, matching the water and reflecting sunlight around them. Coral reef fishes often come in bright colors that either match the colors of the reef or help them to stand out against the colors of the reef. Species that live among underwater plants tend to be greenish, those that live on sand are often tan, and fishes of muddy bottoms tend to be gray or brown.

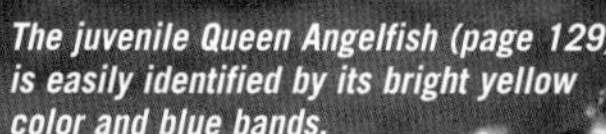

The juvenile Queen Angelfish (page 129) is easily identified by its bright yellow color and blue bands.

The Sergeant Major (page 130) has bars of color.

BANDS, BARS, AND BLOTCHES

Most fishes have patterns of some sort, such as spots or stripes. Bands of color that run vertically—that is, down the fish's side from the back to the belly—are called bars. Broad, lengthwise bands, running from head to tail, are called stripes. Narrow stripes are called lines. Sharply outlined dots of color are called spots, but those with fuzzy edges are called blotches.

The White Shark (page 53) is countershaded.

DARK ON TOP, LIGHT BELOW

Most fishes are darker on top than on the bottom. This is called countershading. It makes the fish harder to see in open water. Fishes that spend most of their time near the surface may be blue on top and white below. If a predator is above looking down, the blue blends in with the blue of the water. If the predator is below looking upward, the pale belly matches the light coming from the sky, making the prey hard to see.

The Mottled Sculpin (page 142) has a mottled pattern of indistinct blotches that helps it blend in with its rocky habitat.

Conservation

Fishes and human beings both depend on water. People need water for drinking and cooking, for irrigating food crops, for transportation, and for disposing of wastes. All of these uses by people can cause changes in fish habitats, and the result can force certain fishes from their native waters and even endanger the survival of the species.

POLLUTION

Pollution from farms, factories, and electric power companies is a serious threat to fishes. Fertilizers and pesticides from farms run off into waters and can kill fishes and other creatures that share the habitat. Pollution that harms fishes affects people, too, because we share the water with the fishes of the world.

Laws about pollution have helped improve the quality of waters in North America, but it takes many years to repair the damage—some habitats will never recover.

Sea Lamprey (page 50)

INTRODUCED SPECIES

Still another threat to native species is the introduction of foreign fishes into native habitats. Sometimes the newcomers are predators or competitors that have been able to take over and exclude the native species. The Sea Lamprey has been introduced to North American freshwater habitats and has devastated native species of fish.

CONSTRUCTION AND DESTRUCTION

Some fishes spawn in special areas like small streams and coastal marshes. When these habitats are filled in to build houses for people, or factories, the fish lose their homes. As a result, many fishes that once were widespread are now endangered species.

The Colorado Pikeminnow (page 67) was once common in the southwestern U.S. Dams on the Colorado River have endangered this species.

Overfishing

Another problem for fishes is that people have overfished species that are good to eat. So many fish have been caught that not enough have been left to reproduce and maintain the population—species that were once abundant have become scarce. Overfishing of Swordfish in the Atlantic and Pacific oceans has seriously depleted the populations of these beautiful fishes.

BE A FRIEND TO FISHES

No one alone can solve the problems of fish conservation, but you can begin by getting involved with nature and wildlife organizations. If you go fishing, another way to help is to release the fish you catch and always be respectful of their habitats while you are observing them.

Gently release the fish you catch.

Using the field guide

Brook Trout
page 80

This section features 50 common North American fishes and includes brief descriptions of 146 more. Color photographs and details about each fish are included to help you identify it. Fishes appearing on facing pages together are either related or share some traits or characteristics.

ICONS

These icons appear on each left-hand page in the field guide. They identify a fish's general shape and category.

Eels and lampreys

Sharks

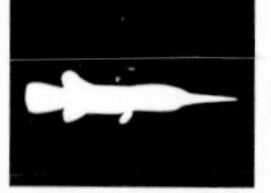

Gars and pikes

Sunfishes and basses

Flatfishes

Snappers and jacks

Puffers and toadfishes

Damselfishes

Rays and skates

Minnows, trouts, perches, and catfishes

SHAPE ICON
This icon identifies the featured fish's general shape and category.

NAME
Each fish's common and scientific names appear here.

BOX HEADING
The box heading alerts you to other fishes covered in the box that are similar to the main fish on the page.

NURSE SHARK
Ginglymostoma cirratum

Sharks are called cartilaginous fishes because their skeletons are made of cartilage, a softer material than true bone. Their fins have many fine rays and many have tails shaped like crescent moons. Sharks are elongate fishes with five to seven pairs of gill slits on the side of the head, mostly above the level of the pectoral fins. The Nurse Shark is relatively common and is frequently seen by snorkelers. It is one of the few sharks that rests motionless on the bottom, often with its head under a rocky ledge.

LOOK FOR: A brownish-green, elongate shark with dorsal and anal fins far back and nearly the same size. Barbels near nostrils.

LENGTH: 14'.

HABITAT: Shallow coastal waters, frequently around mangroves or near rocky shelter.

RANGE:

OTHER SHARKS

LEMON SHARK
Negaprion brevirostris
LOOK FOR: A yellowish-brown shark. Dorsal fins nearly equal in size. **LENGTH:** 10'. **HABITAT:** Shallow coastal waters. **RANGE:** New Jersey to Brazil; Gulf of California to Ecuador. **CAUTION:** Known to attack swimmers.

WHITE SHARK
Carcharodon carcharius
LOOK FOR: A large, gray shark with a white belly. Dusky blotch behind pectoral fin. Large, triangular teeth. Small second dorsal fin. **LENGTH:** 26'. **HABITAT:** Warm oceans, coastal waters. **RANGE:** Pacific and Atlantic oceans. **CAUTION:** Known to attack swimmers.

SPINY DOGFISH
Squalus acanthias
LOOK FOR: A small shark with a strong, hard spine before each dorsal fin. No anal fin. Gray with white spots, lighter below. **LENGTH:** 4'. **HABITAT:** Cold coastal waters. **RANGE:** Pacific and Atlantic coasts.

53

DENTIFICATION CAPSULE
he identification apsule covers all the etails you need to dentify a fish: color, ize, shape, and other eatures described in his book.

RANGE AND HABITAT
The range and habitat listings tell you whether or not a fish is likely to be seen in your area. Areas colored blue indicate native range and areas colored yellow indicate where people have introduced a species of fish.

CAUTION
A caution listing alerts you to a fish that may be dangerous. Handle all fishes with care—many have sharp teeth and spikes that can harm you.

Sea Lamprey

Petromyzon marinus

Lampreys are among the oldest fishes on earth. These long, eel-shaped fishes survive by feeding off the blood of other fishes. They have mouths like suction cups, which they use to attach themselves to other fishes. With the teeth on their tongues, they scrape a hole in their victim's skin and feed. Sea Lampreys live in salt water but spawn in freshwater streams where they build nests of pebbles. After spawning, the adults die. The young lampreys swim downstream and bury themselves in the mud, where they live for several years. As they transform into adults, they develop eyes and teeth and become parasites.

Look for: An eel-shaped lamprey with 7 pairs of round gill openings, suckerlike mouth, and 2 separate dorsal fins. Males gray with orange splotches and fatty ridge in front of dorsal fins.

Length: 24".

Habitat: Adults in open ocean; larvae in mud. Spawns in freshwater streams with gravel bottoms.

Range:

MOUTH

AMERICAN BROOK LAMPREY

Lampetra appendix

LOOK FOR: A small lamprey with 2 dorsal fins and 7 pairs of gill openings. Mouth has only a few patches of tiny teeth. **LENGTH:** 10". **HABITAT:** Small to midsize freshwater streams. **RANGE:** Eastern North America.

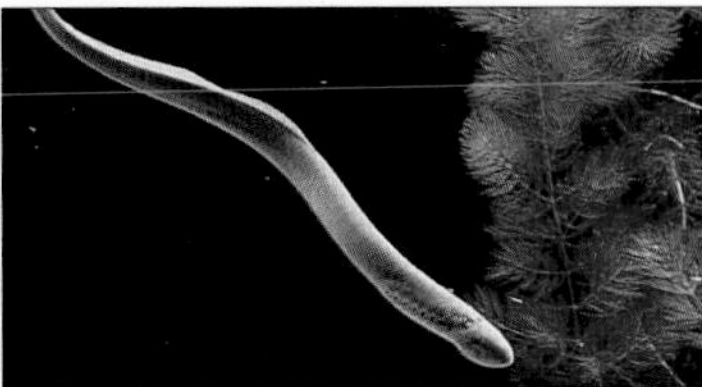

SILVER LAMPREY

Ichthyomyzon unicuspis

LOOK FOR: A small lamprey with a single, notched dorsal fin. Well-developed teeth. **LENGTH:** 12". **HABITAT:** Spawns in small streams; adults live in lakes or large rivers. **RANGE:** North-central U.S.

ATLANTIC HAGFISH

Myxine glutinosa

LOOK FOR: An eel-shaped fish with barbels around nostril and mouth. 1 nostril and 1 gill opening. Secretes slime along lower side. **LENGTH:** 31". **HABITAT:** Muddy ocean bottoms at depths of 90–1,500'. **RANGE:** Newfoundland to New York.

NURSE SHARK
Ginglymostoma cirratum

Sharks are called cartilaginous fishes because their skeletons are made of cartilage, a softer material than true bone. Their fins have many fine rays and many have tails shaped like crescent moons. Sharks are elongate fishes with five to seven pairs of gill slits on the side of the head, mostly above the level of the pectoral fins. The Nurse Shark is relatively common and is frequently seen by snorkelers. It is one of the few sharks that rests motionless on the bottom, often with its head under a rocky ledge.

LOOK FOR: A brownish-green, elongate shark with dorsal and anal fins far back and nearly the same size. Barbels near nostrils.

LENGTH: 14'.

HABITAT: Shallow coastal waters, frequently around mangroves or near rocky shelter.

RANGE:

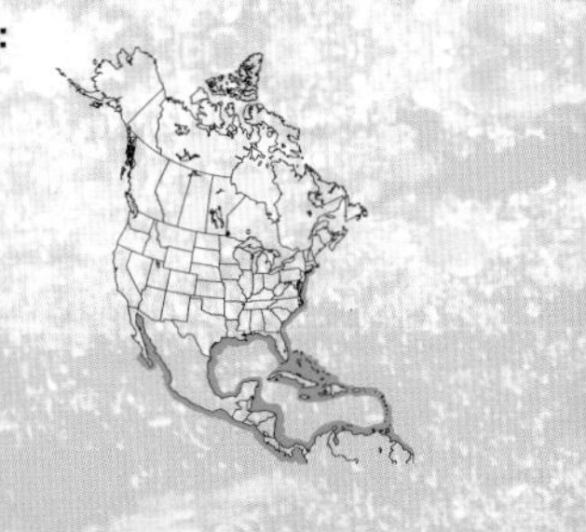

LEMON SHARK
Negaprion brevirostris

LOOK FOR: A yellowish-brown shark. Dorsal fins nearly equal in size. **LENGTH:** 10'. **HABITAT:** Shallow coastal waters. **RANGE:** New Jersey to Brazil; Gulf of California to Ecuador. **CAUTION:** Known to attack swimmers.

WHITE SHARK
Carcharodon carcharius

LOOK FOR: A large, gray shark with a white belly. Dusky blotch behind pectoral fin. Large, triangular teeth. Small second dorsal fin. **LENGTH:** 26'. **HABITAT:** Warm oceans, coastal waters. **RANGE:** Pacific and Atlantic oceans. **CAUTION:** Known to attack swimmers.

SPINY DOGFISH
Squalus acanthias

LOOK FOR: A small shark with a strong, hard spine before each dorsal fin. No anal fin. Gray with white spots; lighter below. **LENGTH:** 4'. **HABITAT:** Cold coastal waters. **RANGE:** Pacific and Atlantic coasts.

ATLANTIC STINGRAY

Dasyatis sabina

Skates and rays are among the most unusual and impressive fishes in the world. Known as batoids, they are flattened, cartilaginous fishes with wide pectoral fins, which they can flap like wings. Together with the body, these fins give the batoids their characteristic disk shape. Batoids are usually measured by their width, not their length. The Atlantic Stingray has five pairs of gill slits on the underside of the pectoral fins. It gets the "sting" in its name from a poisonous spine at the base of its tail that can inflict a painful, stinging wound.

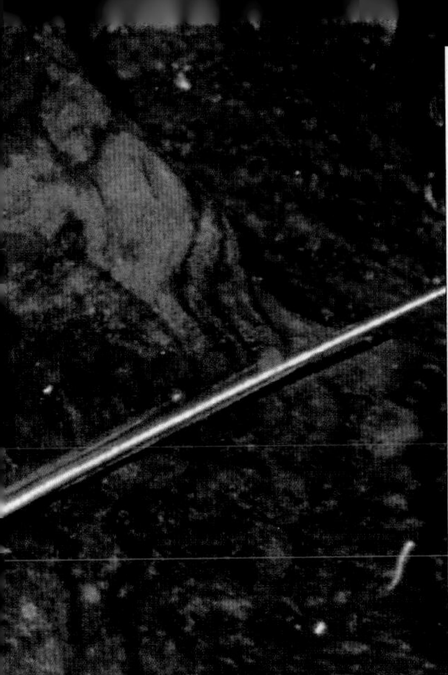

LOOK FOR: A small, flat ray with a rounded body and a snout ending in a short point. Long, slender tail without fin. Saw-edged spine near base of tail.

WIDTH OF DISK: Males 8"; females 24".

HABITAT: Shallow coastal waters; freshwater streams near coast.

RANGE:

CAUTION: Stingrays have a poisonous "stinger" near their tails. Watch out!

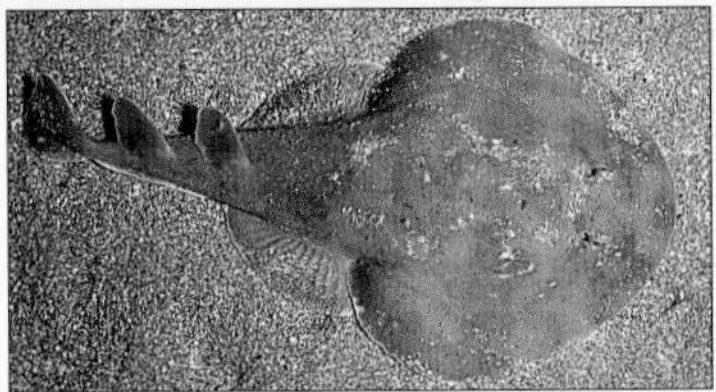

LESSER ELECTRIC RAY

Narcine brasiliensis

LOOK FOR: A sand-colored ray with a rounded body, 2 dorsal fins, and triangular tail fin. Can give electric shock to jolt its prey and predators. **WIDTH OF DISK:** 18". **HABITAT:** Shoreline waters to depths of 130'. **RANGE:** North Carolina to West Indies, Gulf of Mexico.

CLEARNOSE SKATE

Raja eglanteria

LOOK FOR: A ray with dark bars on upper side. Small, narrow tail fin. **WIDTH OF DISK:** 18". **HABITAT:** Shallow coastal waters. **RANGE:** New York to Florida.

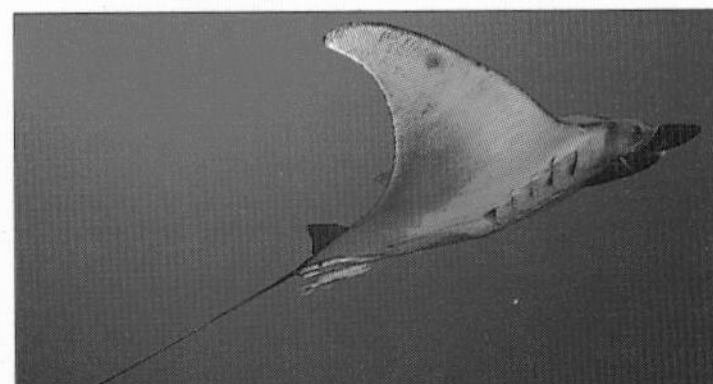

MANTA

Manta birostris

LOOK FOR: A huge, diamond-shaped ray. Large flap on each side of mouth. **WIDTH OF DISK:** 20'. **HABITAT:** Warm open ocean, coastlines. **RANGE:** North Carolina to Brazil, Bermuda, Gulf of Mexico.

Atlantic Sturgeon

Acipenser oxyrhynchus

In the right conditions, sturgeons can live to be as old as most people, if not older: One was estimated to be 154 years old. Sturgeons are bony fishes with mostly cartilaginous skeletons and sharklike fins. Large and elongate, they have five rows of bony, pointed plates, called scutes, along the body. The Atlantic Sturgeon swims along the ocean bottom and feels for its food with four long barbels on its cone-shaped snout. Many aquariums have sturgeons on display.

Look for: A large sturgeon with a wide mouth located on the underside of its head. Olive or gray above, lighter below.

Length: 6'.

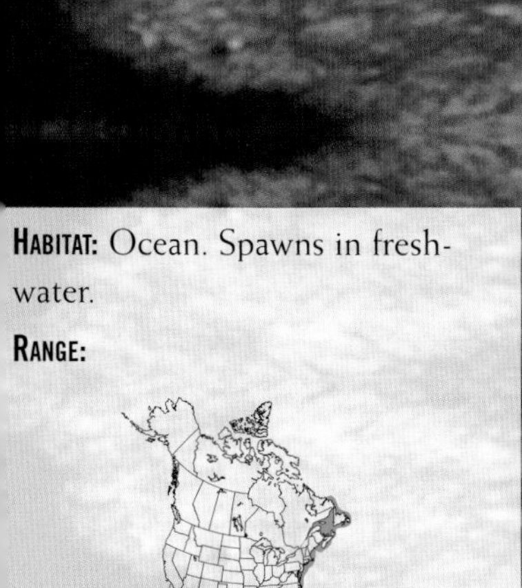

HABITAT: Ocean. Spawns in freshwater.

RANGE:

LAKE STURGEON
Acipenser fulvescens

LOOK FOR: A freshwater sturgeon with a broad mouth, about ¾ as wide as its head. Juveniles light brown with black blotches. Adults dark gray; can weigh more than 300 lbs. **LENGTH:** 8'. **HABITAT:** Lakes, larger rivers. **RANGE:** South-central Canada, north-central U.S.

PADDLEFISH
Polyodon spathula

LOOK FOR: An elongate fish with smooth, scaleless skin and a pointed gill cover. Long, flat, paddle-shaped snout and large mouth with many fine gill rakers. Closely related to sturgeons but has no scales or scutes. **LENGTH:** 5'. **HABITAT:** Large rivers, often with changing water levels. Spawns upstream; sometimes gets stuck below dams. **RANGE:** Lower Mississippi River and tributaries, Gulf of Mexico drainages.

Longnose Gar

Lepisosteus osseus

Gars are an ancient family of bony fishes that were once widespread but are now confined to about seven species in North and Central America. Gars are easily recognized by their elongate shape, very hard, diamond-shaped scales, and extended snouts with sharp teeth. Gars are able to breathe air by swimming at the surface and gulping air into their specialized swim bladders. Longnose Gars can often be seen floating near the water's surface. Their eggs are poisonous to predators.

Look for: A brownish gar. Dorsal and anal fins far back; tail rounded, with slanted base. Juveniles have dark line along each side.

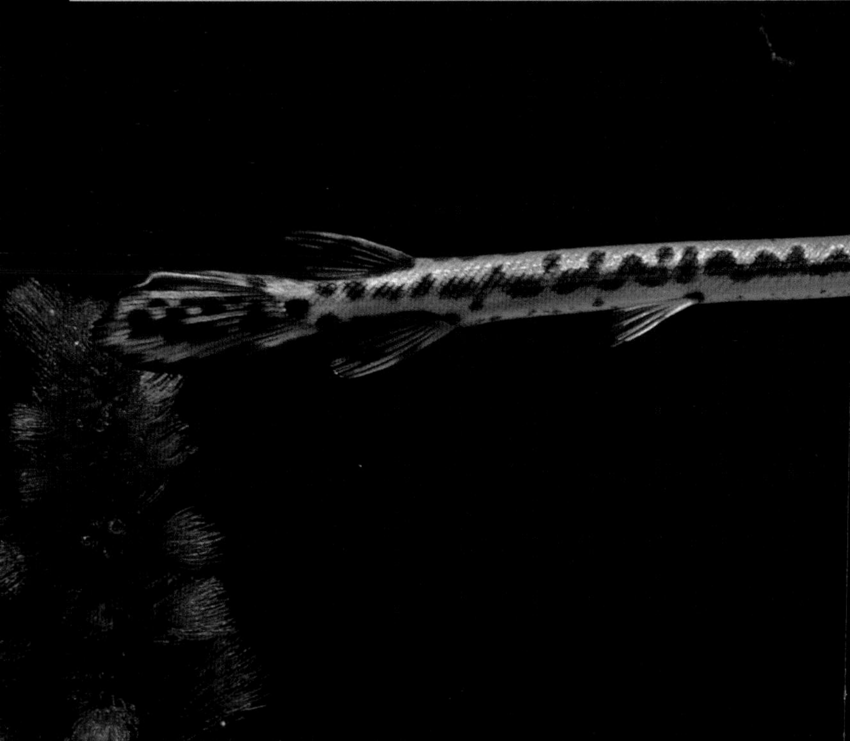

LENGTH: 3–6'.

HABITAT: Lakes and slow-moving streams with dense vegetation.

RANGE:

ALLIGATOR GAR

Atractosteus spatula

LOOK FOR: A very large, plain, grayish gar with a broad snout. **LENGTH:** 10'. **HABITAT:** Large rivers. **RANGE:** Southern Illinois and Ohio to western Florida, south to Vera Cruz, Mexico, lower reaches of Gulf of Mexico drainages.

SPOTTED GAR

Lepisosteus oculatus

LOOK FOR: A small gar with a moderately long snout and round, black spots on top of head. **LENGTH:** 30". **HABITAT:** Lakes, slow-moving streams. **RANGE:** Western Lake Erie, Illinois to northern Mississippi River Valley, Texas to western Florida.

BOWFIN

Amia calva

LOOK FOR: A heavy-bodied greenish fish with a bony, bullet-shaped head. Large, thin scales. Long dorsal fin. Spot at upper base of tail. **LENGTH:** 24". **HABITAT:** Lakes, slow-moving streams. **RANGE:** Central North America.

Tarpon

Megalops atlanticus

The Tarpon is a popular sportfish known for spectacular leaps when caught on a hook and line. These silvery fish spawn in estuaries. As adults, they travel to deeper, coastal salt water, where they can grow quite large. Some Tarpon have weighed in at over 300 pounds! Like eels, Tarpon, Ladyfish, and Bonefish go through a plankton stage as they mature.

Look for: A large, spindle-shaped fish with large, silvery scales and bony jaws. Last ray of dorsal fin long and threadlike; deeply forked tail fin.

Length: 8′.

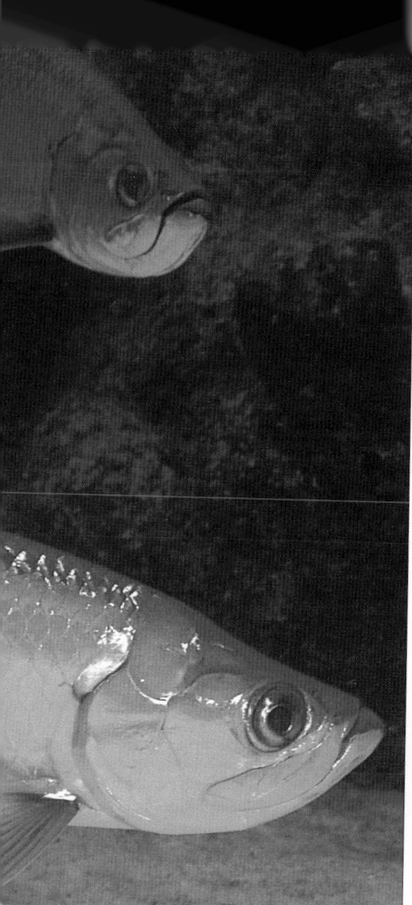

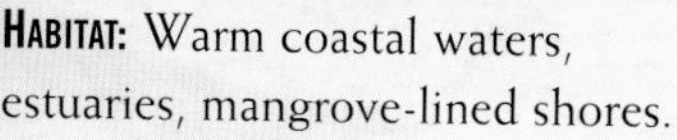

Habitat: Warm coastal waters, estuaries, mangrove-lined shores.

Range:

Ladyfish

Elops saurus

Look for: A slightly compressed, spindle-shaped fish with large eyes. Body silver overall with blue shading above and yellowish below. **Length:** 3'. **Habitat:** Shallow coastal waters. **Range:** Atlantic coast to Brazil, West Indies, and Gulf of Mexico.

Bonefish

Albula vulpes

Look for: A silvery-white, round-bodied, spindle-shaped fish with a conical snout that overhangs the mouth. Single dorsal fin without spines. **Length:** 3'5". **Habitat:** Shallow, tropical salt waters with mud and sand bottoms, around mangroves. **Range:** Pacific and Atlantic coasts.

American Eel

Anguilla rostrata

If you see a fish that looks like a snake underwater, you've probably spotted an eel. Most of the 15 different families of eels in the world live in salt water. The American Eel lives in fresh water but swims out to the open ocean to spawn. No one has actually seen an adult eel spawning, but scientists think these eels lay their eggs near Bermuda in the Sargasso Sea. As they mature into elvers (young eels), they come closer to the coast. The males remain in shallow estuaries, while the females migrate into fresh water. After many years, the adults return to the sea to spawn.

LOOK FOR: An eel with large pectoral fins. Dorsal and anal fins connected to a well-developed tail. Lower jaw longer than upper. Tiny, separate scales form basket-weave pattern.

LENGTH: Females 4'; males smaller.

HABITAT: Atlantic drainages, shallow coastal waters, freshwater streams. Spawns in open ocean.

RANGE:

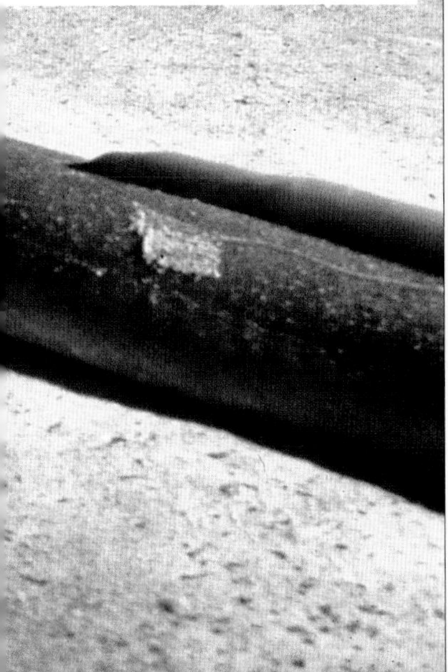

GOLDSPOTTED SNAKE EEL

Myrichthys ocellatus

LOOK FOR: A saltwater eel that has a sharply pointed tail without a tail fin or with a tiny tail fin. Sides have dark blotches with a golden spot at center. **LENGTH:** 3'. **HABITAT:** Coral reefs. **RANGE:** Bermuda, West Indies, south to Brazil.

GREEN MORAY

Gymnothorax funebris

LOOK FOR: A large, heavy-bodied saltwater eel. Plain green. No pectoral fins. **LENGTH:** 6'. **HABITAT:** Coral reefs, rocks, and other shelter. **RANGE:** New Jersey to Brazil, Bermuda, West Indies. **CAUTION:** Some reports of attacks on snorkelers.

Gizzard Shad

Dorosoma cepedianum

Whether swimming in the ocean in schools or squeezed into a tin can at the deli, most herrings seem to come in groups. These compressed, silvery fishes have a single dorsal fin and no spines. Most herrings live in the ocean, but a few can be seen in North American fresh waters. Some species like the American Shad migrate into freshwater streams to spawn. The Gizzard Shad spends most of its time in large schools cruising for food. Gizzard Shad have a special stomach which grinds up plants and small animals it finds in muddy bottoms of lakes and streams.

Look for: A freshwater herring with a deep, silvery, compressed body. Last ray of dorsal fin long and threadlike.

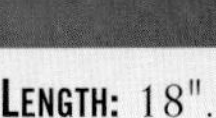

Length: 18".

Habitat: Freshwater lakes and streams.

Range:

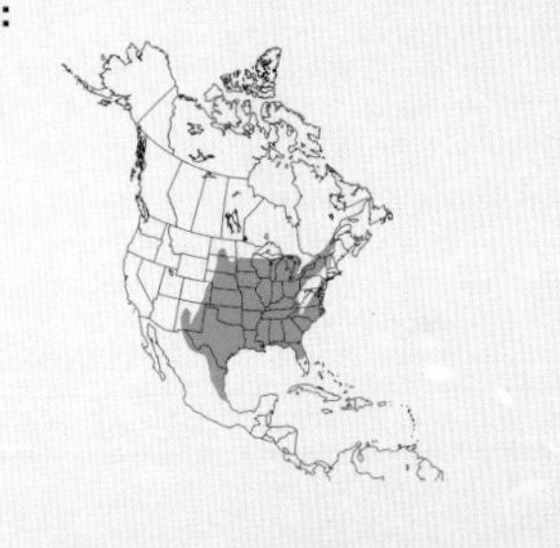

Alewife

Alosa pseudoharengus

Look for: A small, elongate herring with a compressed body. Last ray of dorsal fin is short. Introduced into many lakes. **Length:** Marine 12"; freshwater 6". **Habitat:** Coasts, some lakes. Spawns in streams. **Range:** Newfoundland to South Carolina.

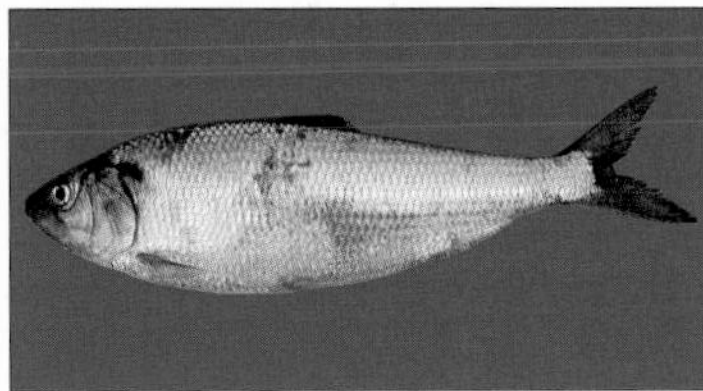

American Shad

Alosa sapidissima

Look for: A large, silvery herring with a deep, compressed body. Important food fish. **Length:** 20". **Habitat:** Oceans. Spawns in freshwater rivers and streams. **Range:** Newfoundland to Florida.

Bay Anchovy

Anchoa mitchilli

Look for: A small anchovy with a conical snout overhanging a very large mouth. **Length:** 4". **Habitat:** Coastal shores, estuaries. **Range:** Maine to Yucatán, Mexico.

Common Carp

Cyprinus carpio

Minnows are the largest fish family in North America, with more than 230 species. Most minnows are small, and many species look alike. Minnows have no teeth in their mouths; instead they grind their food with highly specialized teeth in their throats. During the breeding season, the males of many minnow species develop small, hornlike points called breeding tubercles. The size and location of these tubercles can be useful in recognizing species. Minnows are seen in many lakes and streams in North America. The Common Carp is a Eurasian minnow that was introduced into the United States in the early 1800s. It is still often used as food.

Look for: A thick, heavy-bodied minnow with large scales and 2 pairs of barbels on upper jaw. Strong, saw-edged, spinelike bony

rays at front of dorsal and anal fins.

LENGTH: 2–4'.

HABITAT: Lakes, ponds, slow-moving streams.

RANGE:

GOLDFISH

Carassius auratus

LOOK FOR: An olive to brilliant reddish-orange minnow with large scales and no barbels. Saw-edged spines at front of dorsal and anal fins. Reaches large sizes in the wild. **LENGTH:** 12–14". **HABITAT:** Ponds, slow-moving streams. **RANGE:** Introduced throughout North America.

GRASS CARP

Ctenopharyngodon idella

LOOK FOR: A large minnow with big scales, a short dorsal fin, and no barbels. Stocked to control weeds in ponds. **LENGTH:** 4'. **HABITAT:** Streams, lakes, ponds. **RANGE:** Introduced throughout the U.S.

COLORADO PIKEMINNOW

Ptychocheilus lucius

LOOK FOR: A large, elongate minnow with a large mouth. Endangered. **LENGTH:** 24". **HABITAT:** Midsize streams; juveniles in quieter backwaters. **RANGE:** Colorado River basin.

Creek Chub

Semotilus atromaculatus

In North America there are many native and introduced minnows. Fish of the minnow family are also called shiners, chubs, dace, and carps. A few large breeding tubercles (small, hornlike points) develop on the head of the male Creek Chub, earning this species the name Horned Dace in parts of its range.

Look for: A large, round-bodied minnow with a black spot at base of dorsal fin. Tiny barbel in groove above upper lip. Juveniles have dark stripe along each side.

Length: 12".

HABITAT: Freshwater streams.

RANGE:

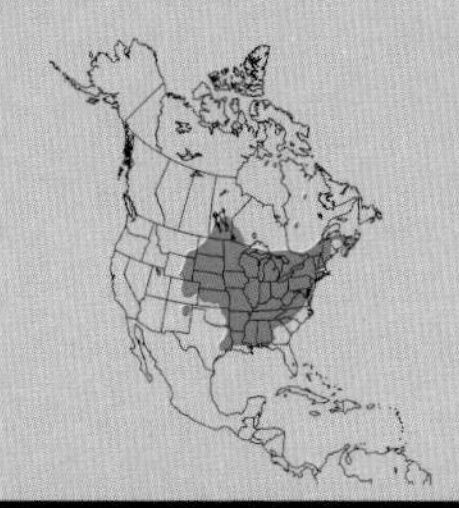

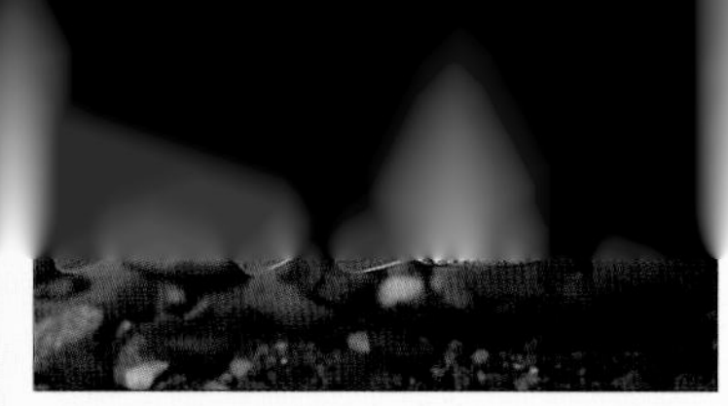

RIVER CHUB
Nocomis micropogon

LOOK FOR: A minnow with large scales and 1 barbel at end of upper jaw. Eyes small. Moves pebbles with mouth to make large nests that are easily seen in streambeds. **LENGTH:** 8". **HABITAT:** Streams. **RANGE:** Great Lakes to northern Alabama and Mississippi.

CENTRAL STONEROLLER
Campostoma anomalum

LOOK FOR: An elongate minnow with a cartilaginous ridge on lower jaw used to scrape food from rock surfaces. **LENGTH:** 9". **HABITAT:** Streams. **RANGE:** Central U.S.

CUTLIPS MINNOW
Exoglossum maxillingua

LOOK FOR: A thick, waxy, olive-colored minnow. Lower jaw has sharp blade used to cut out eyes of other fishes for food. 2 fleshy lobes on each side of jaw. **LENGTH:** 5". **HABITAT:** Streams. **RANGE:** Southeastern Canada to Virginia.

Striped Shiner

Notropis chrysocephalus

Shiners, members of the minnow family, get their name from their silvery scales. There are many kinds of shiners, and some can be difficult to identify. In the spring, males of some species develop beautiful breeding colors and complex patterns of breeding tubercles. The Striped Shiner occurs abundantly throughout its range. Anglers often use it as bait for catching basses and other fishes.

Look for: A compressed, silvery-scaled minnow with dark patches. Breeding males have bright red fins.

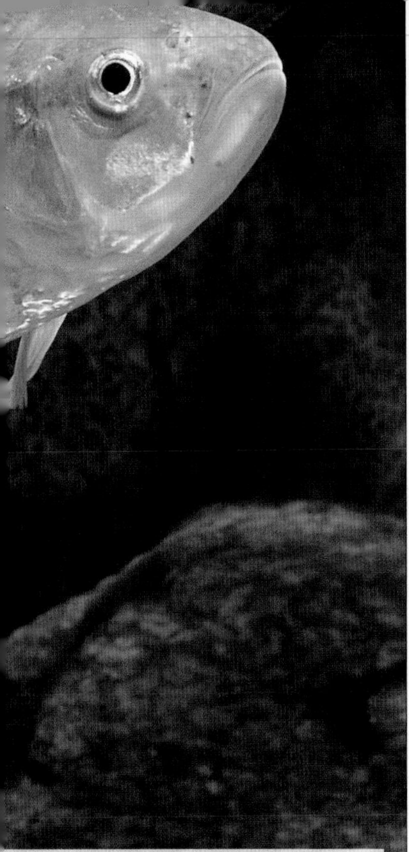

Length: 8".

Habitat: Freshwater streams.

Range:

Spotfin Shiner

Cyprinella spiloptera

Look for: A compressed, streamlined minnow. Firm, diamond-shaped scales with dark margins. Dark coloring on membranes between rays on back of dorsal fin. **Length:** 5". **Habitat:** Lakes, streams. **Range:** North-central U.S.

Spottail Shiner

Notropis hudsonius

Look for: A blunt-nosed minnow with white margin on lower part of tail. **Length:** 5". **Habitat:** Lakes, streams. **Range:** Canada, north-central U.S., Atlantic coast drainages.

Emerald Shiner

Notropis atherinoides

Look for: A slender, compressed minnow. Silvery with a bluish or greenish tinge above. **Length:** 4". **Habitat:** Lakes, large streams. **Range:** North-central Canada to central U.S.

BLUNTNOSE MINNOW

Pimephales notatus

The Bluntnose Minnow is a nest-building species. Males prepare the nest by clearing a small hole beneath a flat rock. The female then deposits the eggs on the underside of the rock, and the male guards them until the young leave the nest.

LOOK FOR: A slender minnow with an overhanging snout. Prominent dark stripe on sides. Scales in front of dorsal fin are small and irregular but have dark edges, so they are easily seen. Spot at front of dorsal fin well above base of fin. Males have a "mustache" of large, pointed breeding tubercles at tip of snout.

LENGTH: 4".

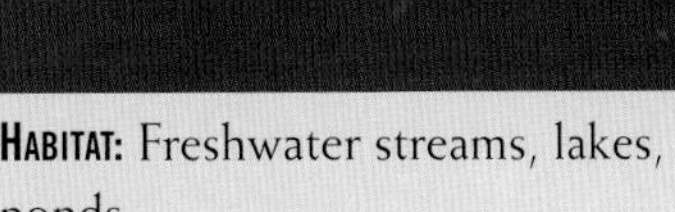

HABITAT: Freshwater streams, lakes, ponds.

RANGE:

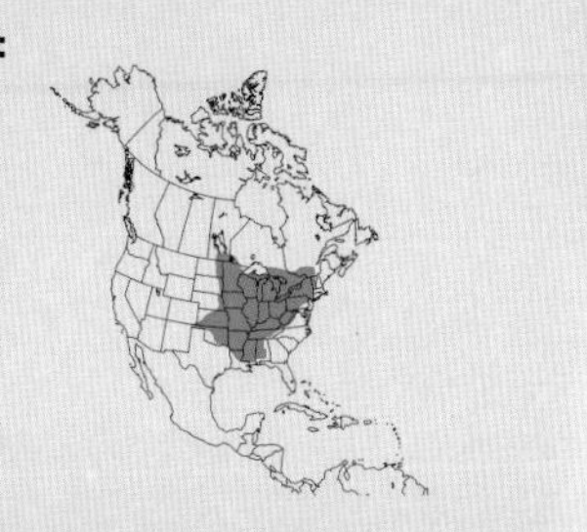

FATHEAD MINNOW

Pimephales promelas

LOOK FOR: A stubby minnow with spot on front of dorsal fin. Scales small, without dark edges. Males have large tubercles on tip of snout. **LENGTH:** 4". **HABITAT:** Streams, lakes, ponds. **RANGE:** Widespread in central North America.

BLACKNOSE DACE

Rhinichthys atratulus

LOOK FOR: A slender minnow with fine scales and dark stripe. Small barbel at corner of mouth. Males have tiny tubercles on back. **LENGTH:** 2". **HABITAT:** Small, cold streams. **RANGE:** Southern Canada, north-central U.S., northern Atlantic coast drainages.

SOUTHERN REDBELLY DACE

Phoxinus erythrogaster

LOOK FOR: A slender minnow with small scales and 2 dark stripes. No barbel on snout. Red belly on breeding males. **LENGTH:** 2½". **HABITAT:** Streams, ponds, lakes; in vegetation. **RANGE:** Mississippi drainages from Wisconsin to Alabama.

White Sucker

Catostomus commersoni

True to their name, these fishes suck in their food—mostly larval insects and other creatures—from the bottoms of freshwater streams and lakes. They have single rows of comblike teeth on bones in their throats. They are closely related to minnows, but their anal fin is farther back and many have short dorsal fins. The White Sucker is extremely common in the eastern United States. Its mouth is on the underside of its head, and it has thick lips covered with fleshy bumps like the tread on an automobile tire.

Look for: An elongate sucker with bumpy lips and scales that are smaller near front of body. Juveniles have 3 blotches on each side.

Length: 24".

HABITAT: Small freshwater creeks to larger rivers, lakes.

RANGE:

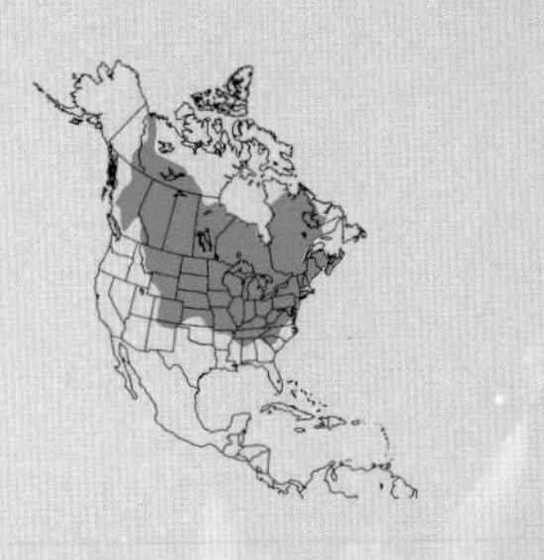

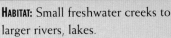

LONGNOSE SUCKER

Catostomus catostomus

LOOK FOR: An elongate sucker with small eyes, a long snout, and fine scales. Often has dark reddish-brown sides. **LENGTH:** 25". **HABITAT:** Streams, lakes. **RANGE:** Southern Canada, northern U.S.

NORTHERN HOG SUCKER

Hypentelium nigricans

LOOK FOR: A round-bodied sucker with a large head that is flattened between the eyes. Often marked with irregular, slanted dark bars. **LENGTH:** 24". **HABITAT:** Clear streams with gravel and rock bottoms. **RANGE:** Central U.S., central Atlantic drainages.

CREEK CHUBSUCKER

Erimyzon oblongus

LOOK FOR: A stubby, small-mouthed sucker. Juveniles have broad, black stripe on side. **LENGTH:** 10". **HABITAT:** Lakes, ponds, slow-moving streams. **RANGE:** East-central U.S., Atlantic coast drainages, around Appalachian Mountains.

Bigmouth Buffalo

Ictiobus cyprinellus

Bigmouth Buffalos are large fishes with a humped back that looks a little bit like the back of a buffalo, hence their common name. Like Quillbacks and other related suckers, Buffalos have long dorsal fins with more than 24 rays. At first glance they resemble carp, but they do not have hard spines in their dorsal and anal fins and have no barbels on the upper jaw.

Look for: A large, gray, deep-bodied, moderately compressed sucker with a long dorsal fin and a large mouth.

Length: 35".

Habitat: Freshwater lakes, large rivers.

RANGE:

BLUE SUCKER

Cycleptus elongatus

LOOK FOR: A very slender, elongate, blue-colored sucker with a long dorsal fin. **LENGTH:** 3'. **HABITAT:** Large rivers, reservoirs. **RANGE:** Larger tributaries of Mississippi River, southern Gulf of Mexico.

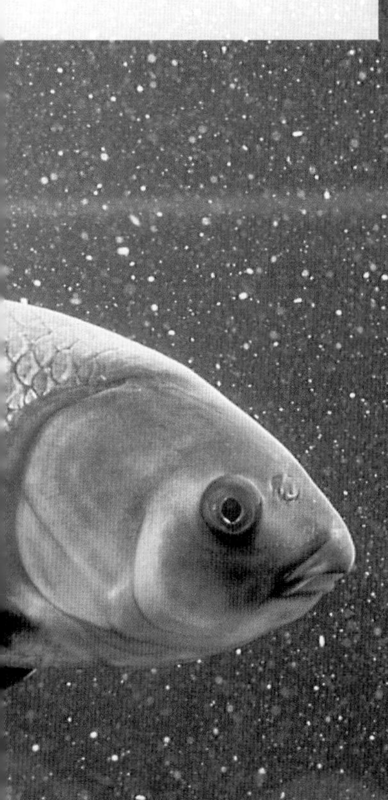

MEXICAN TETRA

Astyanax mexicanus

LOOK FOR: A compressed, silvery fish with an adipose dorsal fin. No belly scutes. Dark streak extending from base of tail fin onto central rays. **LENGTH:** 4". **HABITAT:** Small streams. **RANGE:** New Mexico, southern Texas to Mexico.

Brown Bullhead
Ameiurus nebulosus

Brown Bullhead catfish are easily recognized by their scaleless skin and four pairs of long, slender barbels around the mouth. They have a special fin on their lower back called an adipose fin. They are important sport and food fishes and have been introduced throughout North America. Brown Bullheads have spinelike rays in the pectoral and dorsal fins. Their sticky eggs are deposited in rocky crevices and guarded by the parents for several days after hatching. In the early summer you may see dense clouds of baby Bullheads being guarded by their parents in shallow water.

Look for: A chunky, medium-size catfish with a squarish tail and black chin barbels. Mottled, olive-brown above, lighter below. Large,

irregular "teeth" on pectoral spines.

LENGTH: 18".

HABITAT: Lakes, ponds, slow-moving freshwater streams.

RANGE:

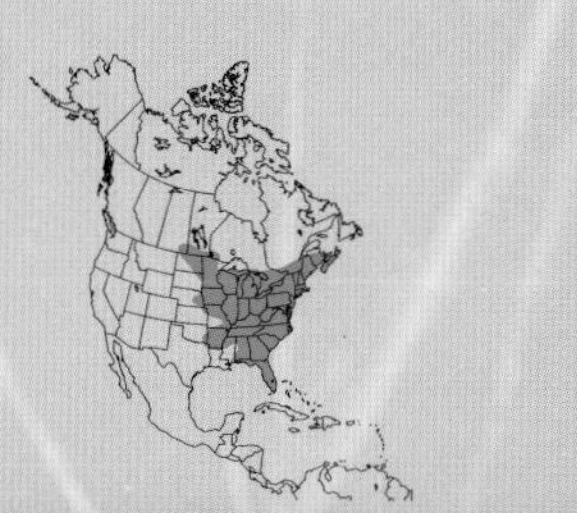

CHANNEL CATFISH

Ictalurus punctatus

LOOK FOR: A large, slender catfish with a forked tail. Blue-gray above, lighter below. Often raised in ponds for food. **LENGTH:** 4'. **HABITAT:** Ponds, lakes, larger streams. **RANGE:** Central North America from southern Canada to Gulf of Mexico coast.

STONECAT

Noturus flavus

LOOK FOR: An elongate catfish. Pale tan with light edge on tail fin and paler areas on back of head and behind dorsal fin. **LENGTH:** 12". **HABITAT:** Streams, lakes, ponds. **RANGE:** North-central U.S., Great Lakes drainages.

HARDHEAD CATFISH

Arius felis

LOOK FOR: An elongate catfish with a forked tail and 2 pairs of barbels on chin but none on snout. Dark-blue above, lighter silvery tones below. **LENGTH:** 14". **HABITAT:** Coastal waters, estuaries. **RANGE:** Cape Cod, Massachusetts, to Yucatán, Mexico.

Brook Trout

Salvelinus fontinalis

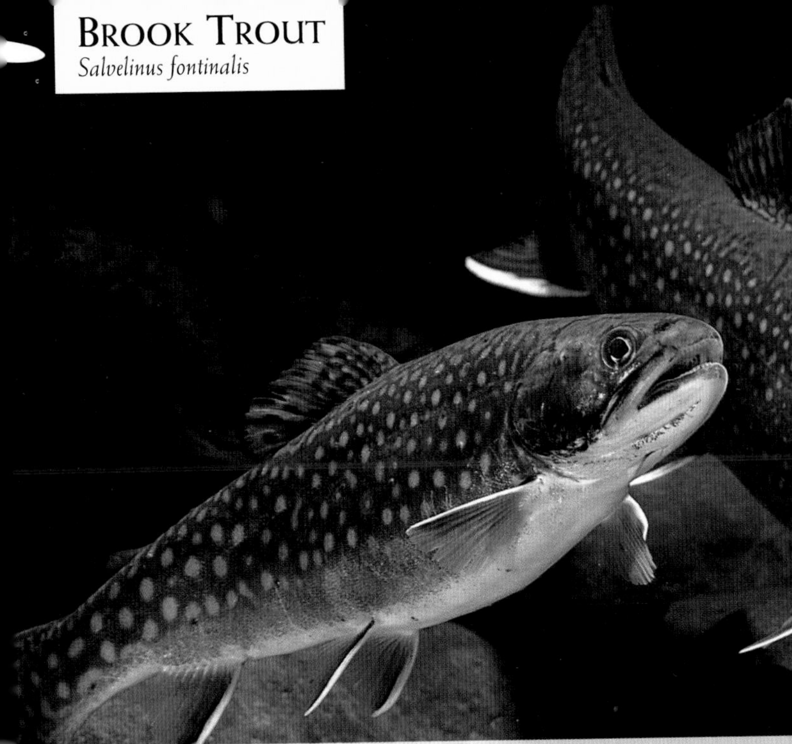

The best place to see trouts and salmons is where anglers flock to try their luck, or at hatcheries where the fishes are raised. Important for both food and sport, these large, handsome fishes have also been extensively introduced in the wild. Trouts live mostly in fresh water and prefer clear, cold streams and lakes, although a few species will occasionally swim into salt water.

Brook Trouts are chars, a kind of trout with very fine scales and light-colored spots. They are among the most colorful freshwater species.

Look for: A colorful, elongate char with a pattern of white spots on a dark background and worm-shaped markings on upper side. Pectoral, pelvic, and anal fins have brilliant white front edges. Tail slightly forked.

LENGTH: 16".

HABITAT: Clear, cool lakes, streams, and very small creeks.

RANGE:

BROWN TROUT

Salmo trutta

LOOK FOR: A pale olive-brown, elongate trout with large, dark spots. Usually no spots on upper half of tail. Introduced from Europe. **LENGTH:** 3'4". **HABITAT:** Colder streams and lakes. **RANGE:** Widely introduced throughout North America.

ATLANTIC SALMON

Salmo salar

LOOK FOR: A silvery salmon with small X-shaped spots. Head and pectoral fins short. Anal fin has 9 rays. Juveniles have dark bars and red spots on sides. **LENGTH:** 4'7". **HABITAT:** Ocean. Spawns in rivers. **RANGE:** Atlantic coast north of Connecticut.

RAINBOW SMELT

Osmerus mordax

LOOK FOR: A rather small, slender fish with an adipose dorsal fin and rough scales. No fin spines. Large, fanglike teeth on tongue. **LENGTH:** 10". **HABITAT:** Ocean and freshwater. **RANGE:** Northern Alaska, Canada, northeastern U.S.

Rainbow Trout
Oncorhynchus mykiss

The striking, speckled Rainbow Trout is native to coastal streams in the western United States but has been widely introduced in the eastern United States and throughout the world. Rainbows that migrate to large lakes or into salt water are silvery all over and are called Steelhead Trout. Although considered a trout, the Rainbow is actually more closely related to salmons.

LOOK FOR: An elongate trout with a pattern of small black spots on a paler background and a pinkish or red stripe along each side.

LENGTH: 3'4".

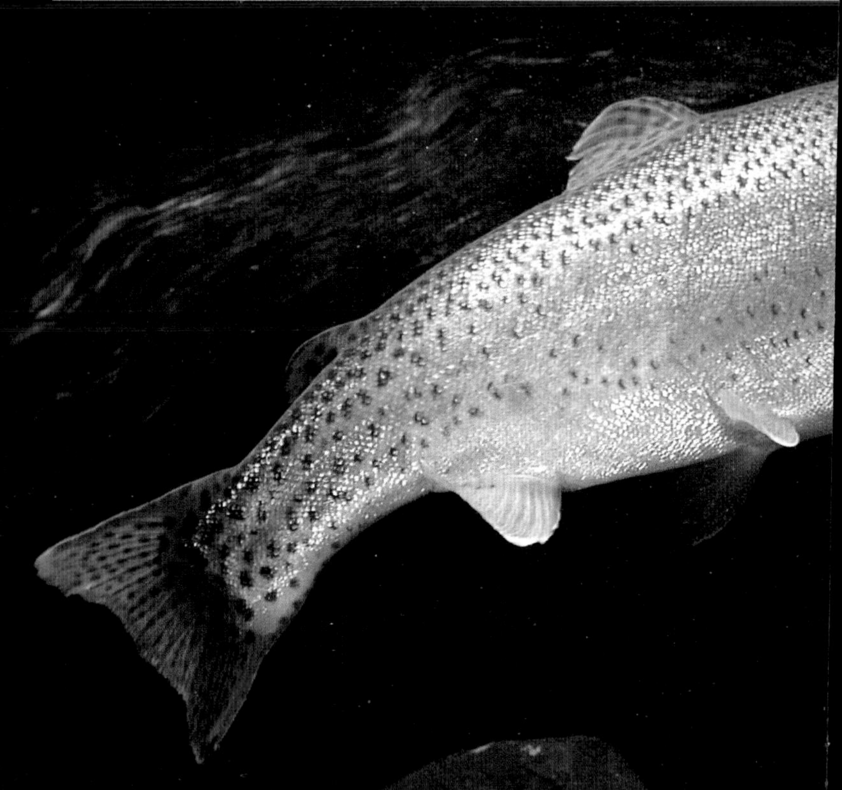

HABITAT: Colder lakes and streams.

RANGE:

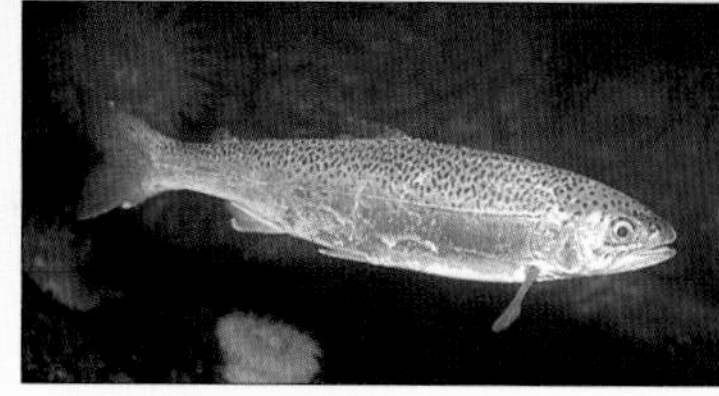

COHO SALMON

Oncorhynchus kisutch

LOOK FOR: A silvery salmon that has a long anal fin with more than 12 rays. Small black spots on upper half of tail fin. Pale gums. **LENGTH:** 3'. **HABITAT:** Ocean, freshwater. Spawns in streams. **RANGE:** Western North America. Introduced into Great Lakes.

LAKE WHITEFISH

Coregonus clupeaformis

LOOK FOR: A large, elongate, silvery-white fish with a snout projecting beyond mouth. Adipose fin. **LENGTH:** 30". **HABITAT:** Cold-water lakes, larger rivers. **RANGE:** Southern Canada, northern U.S.

ARCTIC GRAYLING

Thymallus arcticus

LOOK FOR: An elongate, compressed fish that has a large, bluish dorsal fin with yellow spots. Small mouth, adipose fin. **LENGTH:** 15". **HABITAT:** Clear, cold lakes and streams. **RANGE:** Southern Canada, northern U.S.

Northern Pike

Esox lucius

Pikes and pickerels are a small family (Esocidae) of five species of predatory fishes with slender, elongate bodies and long, sharp teeth. The dorsal and anal fins are far back, the tail is moderately forked, and the mouth is large with the jaws extending forward like the bill of a duck. Esocids live in weedy areas of lakes and streams. Sometimes they can be seen hovering almost motionless near clumps of water plants. The Northern Pike occurs in both North America and Europe. Its large size, enormous appetite, and toothy jaws make it the "shark" of freshwater lakes and streams.

Look for: A large, elongate, greenish pike with creamy white, oval spots on the sides. Cheek and upper half of gill cover scaled.

Length: 4'.

Habitat: Slow-moving, weedy areas in lakes and streams.

Range:

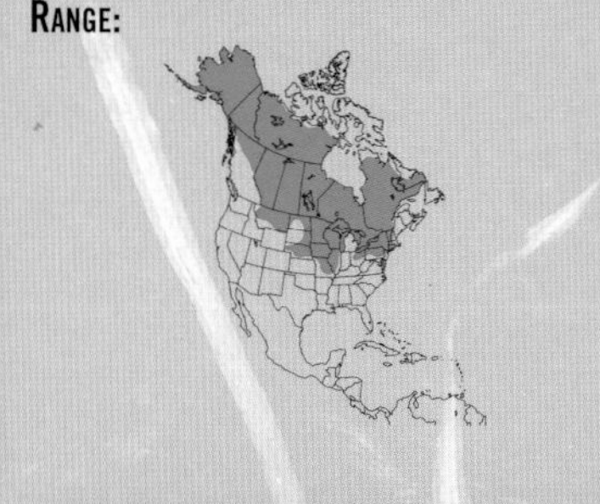

Muskellunge

Esox masquinongy

Look for: A large, greenish-brown fish with no scales on lower part of cheek and gill cover. Color pattern variable. **Length:** 5'4". **Habitat:** Shallow, weedy areas in lakes and larger streams. **Range:** Southern Canada, northeastern U.S.

Grass Pickerel

Esox americanus

Look for: A small pickerel with a short snout. Cheek and gill cover fully scaled. **Length:** 15". **Habitat:** Weedy shorelines of lakes and streams. **Range:** Eastern U.S.

Central Mudminnow

Umbra limi

Look for: A small, brown fish with a dark bar or dumbbell-shaped mark at base of rounded tail. Related to esocids, not minnows. **Length:** 5". **Habitat:** Weedy areas of ponds and streams. **Range:** Southern Canada, north-central U.S.

Trout-Perch

Percopsis omiscomaycus

You might have to stay up late to see a Trout-Perch during the early summer spawning season. This freshwater species waits until night before heading into the shallows to spawn. It is also sometimes seen in large schools over sandy bottoms in streams. Trout-Perch get their name from the fact that they have an adipose fin, like trouts, and true spines in their fins, like perches.

There are two species in North America, the Trout-Perch and the Sand Roller (*Percopsis transmontana*), a similar species that lives in the Columbia River system in Washington, Oregon, and Idaho.

Look for: A small, grayish fish with an adipose fin. Snout overhangs low mouth. Translucent skin with rows of dark spots. Spines at front of dorsal fin. Body tapers evenly toward tail.

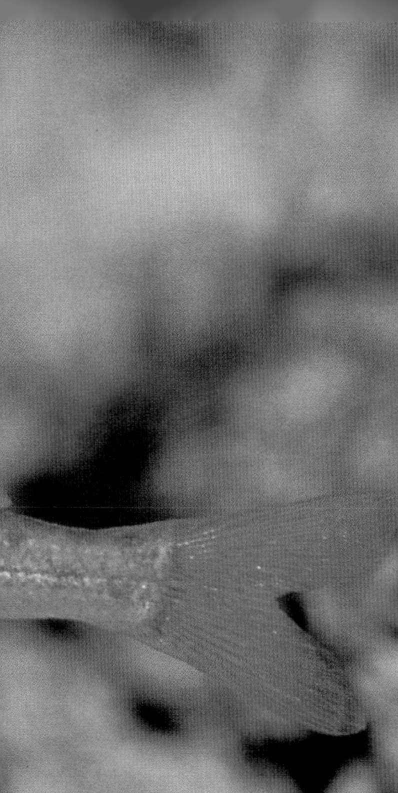

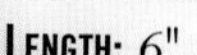

LENGTH: 6".

HABITAT: Freshwater lakes and streams.

RANGE:

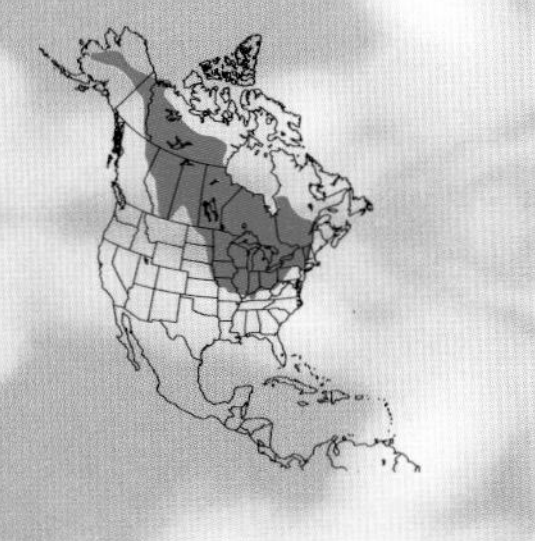

PIRATE PERCH
Aphredoderus sayanus

LOOK FOR: A stubby fish with a squarish tail. Anus of adults located between gill covers. Dark brown or purple to greenish with yellow tones. **LENGTH:** 5½". **HABITAT:** Weedy areas of streams. **RANGE:** Appalachian Mountains, Gulf of Mexico.

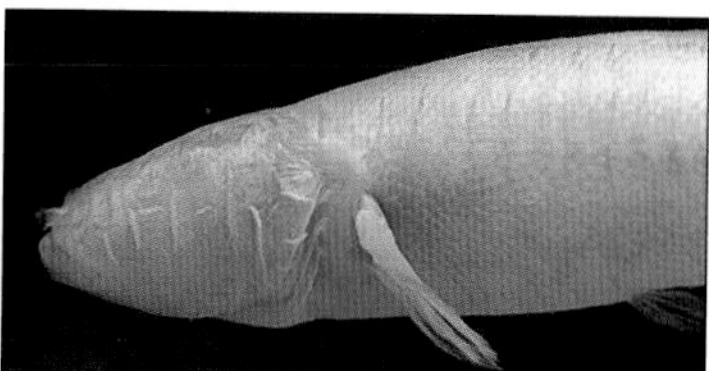

NORTHERN CAVEFISH
Amblyopsis spelaea

LOOK FOR: A slender, pinkish-white fish without eyes. Tiny pelvic fins. **LENGTH:** 4". **HABITAT:** Underground streams and rivers. **RANGE:** Southern Indiana, Kentucky.

SWAMPFISH
Chologaster cornuta

LOOK FOR: A small, slender fish with tiny eyes. Dark above and paler below. Dark line along lower side and dark central area on tail. **LENGTH:** 2". **HABITAT:** Slow-moving freshwater in weedy areas. **RANGE:** Virginia to Georgia.

BURBOT
Lota lota

Codfishes were once such an important source of food for people that they were called the "cows of the sea." Because they have been overfished, codfishes in the North Atlantic are now protected by strict laws. Most species live in salt water, many in very deep parts of the ocean. They have moderately elongate and compressed bodies. The Burbot is a codfish that lives in fresh water. Unlike most fresh water fishes, it spawns on winter nights under the ice in shallow waters, where it leaves its eggs unguarded on clean sand, gravel, or rock bottoms.

LOOK FOR: An elongate codfish with 2 dorsal fins, the first short and the second very long. Rounded tail, long chin barbel. No fin spines.

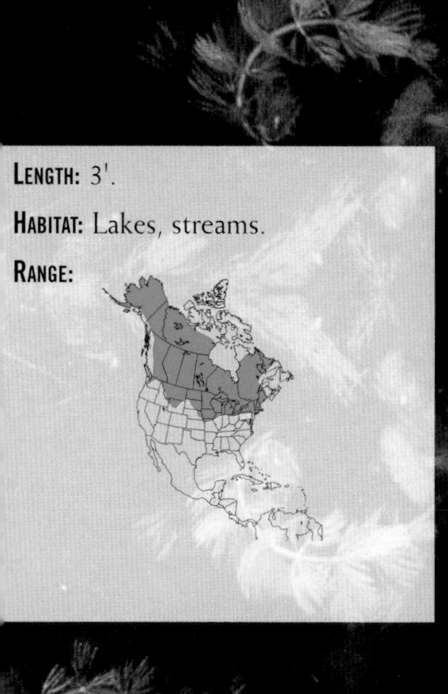

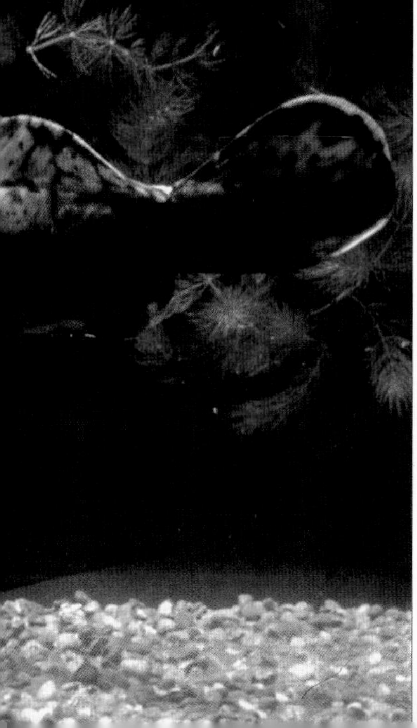

Atlantic Cod

Gadus morhua

LOOK FOR: A brown to grayish-green codfish with 3 dorsal and 2 anal fins. Forked tail. Well-developed chin barbel. Small, dark spots on back. **LENGTH:** 5'. **HABITAT:** Ocean to depths of 200–360' in summer; to 1,200' in winter. **RANGE:** Greenland to North Carolina.

Atlantic Tomcod

Microgadus tomcod

LOOK FOR: A small, elongate codfish with 3 dorsal and 2 anal fins. Tail rounded, front rays of pelvic fins long and threadlike. **LENGTH:** 15". **HABITAT:** Coastal waters, estuaries. **RANGE:** Eastern Canada to New Jersey.

Silver Hake

Merluccius bilinearis

LOOK FOR: A slender codfish with 2 dorsal fins, the second long and notched. Tail forked. No chin barbel. **LENGTH:** 25". **HABITAT:** Ocean to depths of 660' in winter, nearer coast in summer. **RANGE:** Grand Banks, Newfoundland, to South Carolina.

Oyster Toadfish

Opsanus tau

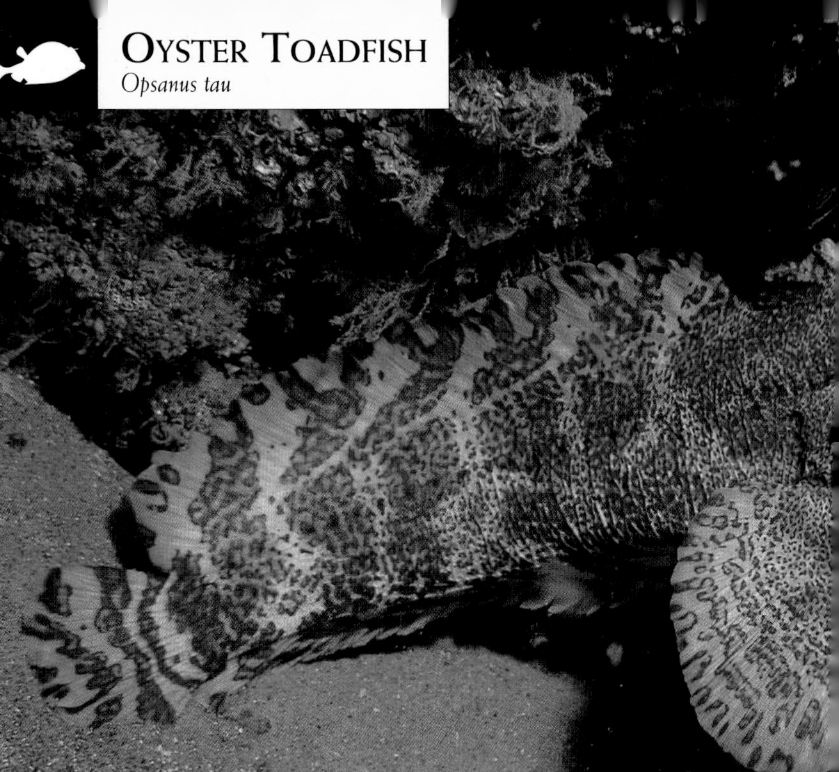

Oyster Toadfish hide on the ocean bottom and snatch their prey by surprise. They are well-camouflaged fish with powerful jaws used to clamp down on their dinner. Most toadfishes have fleshy projections around their mouths, and some produce sounds like boat whistles. Oyster Toadfish have sharp, poisonous spines on their dorsal fin that they can raise when they feel threatened. They spawn in late spring and summer, and the males guard the eggs until they hatch.

Look for: A chunky, compressed toadfish with fleshy projections on its flattened head. First dorsal fin has 3 spines embedded in skin.

Length: 15".

Habitat: Mud, rock, and shell

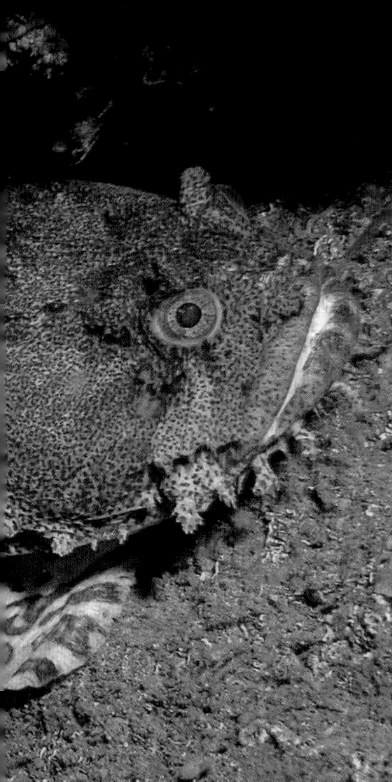

ɔottoms in coastal salt water.

ʀANGE:

.AUTION: All toadfishes should be ıandled carefully if caught.

PLAINFIN MIDSHIPMAN

Porichthys notatus

LOOK FOR: An elongate toadfish that produces light from lines of white spots, called photophores, on its underside. **LENGTH:** 15". **HABITAT:** Shallow salt water. **RANGE:** Alaska to Gulf of California.

GOOSEFISH

Lophius americanus

LOOK FOR: A depressed, brown fish with a huge mouth and long, pointed teeth. "Lure" on first dorsal spine attracts prey. **LENGTH:** 4'. **HABITAT:** Coastal shores to depths of 2,000'. **RANGE:** Gulf of St. Lawrence to Florida.

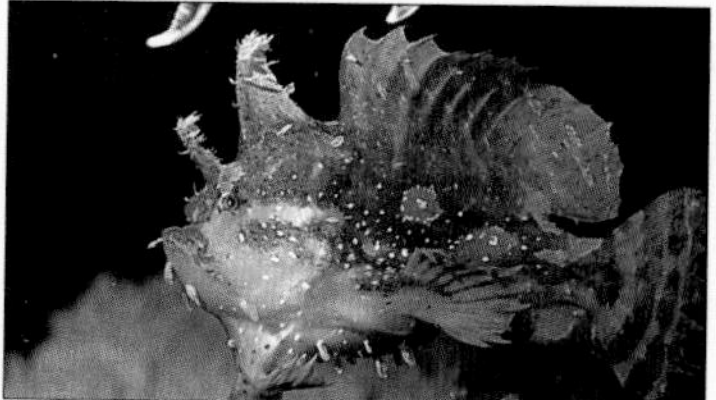

SARGASSUMFISH

Histrio histrio

LOOK FOR: A stubby, compressed fish with limblike pectoral fins. Camouflaged to match floating sargassum weed. **LENGTH:** 6". **HABITAT:** Open ocean in clumps of seaweed. **RANGE:** Pacific and Atlantic oceans.

SQUIRRELFISH
Holocentrus adscensionis

Large eyes are a sure sign of a nocturnal species, and squirrelfishes are no exception. These big-eyed fishes are most active at night, although some species can be seen during the day. They are a common and easy fish to spot if you go snorkeling on coral reefs in Florida or the Caribbean. Squirrelfishes tend to be short and deep-bodied. They are spiny-rayed fishes with strong spines in the dorsal, anal, and pelvic fins. The pelvic fins are far forward, below the pectoral fins.

LOOK FOR: A big-eyed, red fish with strong spines in the dorsal, anal, and tail fins. Deeply forked tail fin with upper lobe longer than lower; base of tail fin slender. Dorsal fin has yellowish center.

Length: 12".

Habitat: Reefs.

Range:

Dusky Squirrelfish

Sargocentron vexillarius

Look for: A small, dark red squirrelfish with black lines on sides. Lower sides darker. **Length:** 7". **Habitat:** Reefs, rocky bottoms among coral branches. **Range:** Florida to Venezuela, Bermuda, West Indies.

Longjaw Squirrelfish

Neoniphon marianus

Look for: A small, red squirrelfish with yellow and white lines. Jutting lower jaw. Spiny dorsal fin yellow with white spots. Large third anal spine. **Length:** 7". **Habitat:** Coral reefs at depths below 45'. **Range:** Florida Keys to West Indies.

Blackbar Soldierfish

Myripristis jacobus

Look for: A red squirrelfish with dark brown band behind gill opening. White edges on dorsal, anal, pelvic, and tail fins. **Length:** 7". **Habitat:** Caves in coral reefs and rocky areas. **Range:** Georgia to Brazil, Bermuda, West Indies.

ATLANTIC FLYINGFISH

Cypselurus melanurus

Flyingfishes make long, flying leaps out of the water, especially when they are chased by hungry predators. These leaps are a defensive tactic—predators can't see them once they are in the air. Their "wings" are in fact pectoral fins that have evolved to become greatly enlarged. Atlantic Flyingfish are elongate, surface-dwelling fish and their lateral line is low on the body. They are greenish or blue above and pale below. They have a single dorsal fin and no fin spines. Their pelvic fins are far back on the body.

LOOK FOR: A 4-winged flyingfish with enlarged pectoral and pelvic fins. Pectoral fins have a pale triangle at the base. Dorsal fin transparent. Both lobes of tail fin dark.

LENGTH: 10".

HABITAT: Ocean waters near surface.

RANGE:

SPOTFIN FLYINGFISH

Cypselurus furatus

LOOK FOR: A 4-winged flyingfish with a dark spot on both pectoral fins. **LENGTH:** 12". **HABITAT:** Ocean waters near surface. **RANGE:** North Carolina to Gulf of Mexico, South America.

BALLYHOO

Hemiramphus brasiliensis

LOOK FOR: An elongate fish with a very long lower jaw and short upper jaw. Tip of lower jaw orange-red. **LENGTH:** 15¾". **HABITAT:** Coastal waters near surface. **RANGE:** Massachusetts to Gulf of Mexico, South America.

ATLANTIC NEEDLEFISH

Strongylura marina

LOOK FOR: A slender, bluish-green fish with jaws of equal length and large, sharp teeth. Silvery below, dark blue stripe on sides. **LENGTH:** 27". **HABITAT:** Coastal waters near surface. **RANGE:** Massachusetts to Gulf of Mexico, South America.

California Grunion

Leuresthes tenuis

The California Grunion spawns on the beaches of the Pacific coast during the high tides of spring and summer. Females may spawn from four to eight times a season. The California Grunion is one of the silversides—a family of slender, elongate fishes with two well-separated dorsal fins, the first of which has four small, slender spines. The silversides get their name from the bright silver stripes along their sides.

LOOK FOR: A large silverside with no teeth or very minute teeth on jaws.

LENGTH: 7¼".

HABITAT: Pacific coastal waters to depths of 60'. Spawns on beaches.

RANGE:

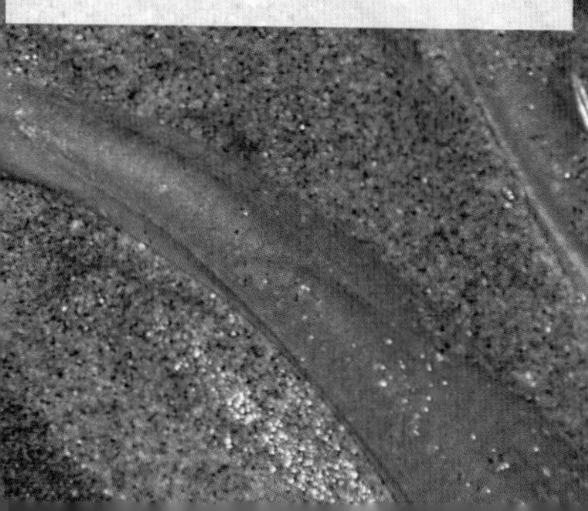

BROOK SILVERSIDE

Labidesthes sicculus

LOOK FOR: An elongate silverside with a bright silvery stripe on both sides. Very small scales and beaklike jaws. **LENGTH:** 5". **HABITAT:** Lakes, ponds, slow-moving parts of streams. **RANGE:** Central U.S., eastern Gulf of Mexico drainages, Florida.

MUMMICHOG

Fundulus heteroclitus

LOOK FOR: A stubby fish with a rounded tail, blunt head, and upturned mouth. **LENGTH:** 5". **HABITAT:** Tidal marshes, estuaries; sometimes in fresh water. **RANGE:** Southern Canada to northeastern Florida.

SHEEPSHEAD MINNOW

Cyprinodon variegatus

LOOK FOR: A short, deep-bodied fish with mottled colors. Not a true minnow. Tolerant of salty water. **LENGTH:** 2". **HABITAT:** Shallow coastal brackish and fresh waters. **RANGE:** Massachusetts to Yucatán, Mexico, and Bahamas.

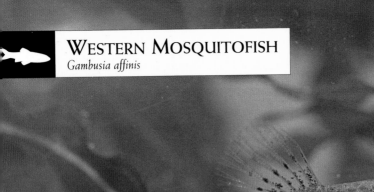

WESTERN MOSQUITOFISH
Gambusia affinis

Mosquitofish are named for their favorite food—pesky mosquitoes! They eat the insects' water-dwelling larvae and are often stocked in order to keep mosquito populations down. Mosquitofish are members of the livebearer family. Male livebearers transfer sperm to females, who then give birth to live young instead of laying eggs. Livebearers are compressed, slender, and sometimes deep-bodied fishes. They have a single dorsal fin, no fin spines, and large smooth scales. Most species have upturned mouths. Females are larger than males.

LOOK FOR: A small, gray livebearer with scales outlined in black.

LENGTH: Females 2"; males 1".

HABITAT: Lakes, ponds, swamps, slow-moving streams.

RANGE:

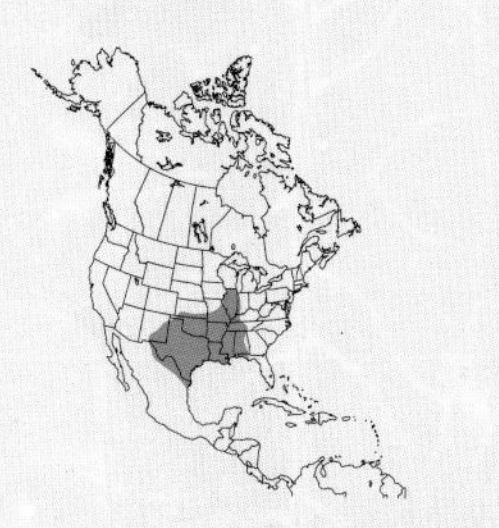

PIKE KILLIFISH

Belonesox belizanus

LOOK FOR: A grayish livebearer with moderately long jaws and strong teeth. Skillfull predator. Tolerant of salt water and low oxygen. **LENGTH:** Females 8"; males 4". **HABITAT:** Slow-moving streams. **RANGE:** Introduced into southern Florida.

SAILFIN MOLLY

Poecilia latipinna

LOOK FOR: A deep-bodied livebearer with a very large dorsal fin. Grayish with rows of spots along sides. **LENGTH:** 4". **HABITAT:** Weedy, slow-moving coastal waters. **RANGE:** North Carolina to Mexico.

LEAST KILLIFISH

Heterandria formosa

LOOK FOR: A small livebearer with black spots on dorsal and anal fins and a black line along sides. **LENGTH:** 1". **HABITAT:** Slow-moving coastal streams and ponds. **RANGE:** North Carolina to Louisiana.

Brook Stickleback

Culaea inconstans

Instead of the first dorsal fin seen on many fishes, the prickly sticklebacks have a row of spines without any connecting skin running down their backs. These sharp spines come in handy, since sticklebacks guard their nests against hungry predators while their eggs hatch. The nests are built by the males out of bits of vegetation they find in the water. Sticklebacks live in weedy shallows and can be fairly easy to see. They are small, generally elongate fishes with a tiny mouth at the end of a long face. The base of the tail fin is long and slender.

Look for: A small, mottled, greenish stickleback with 5 dorsal spines.

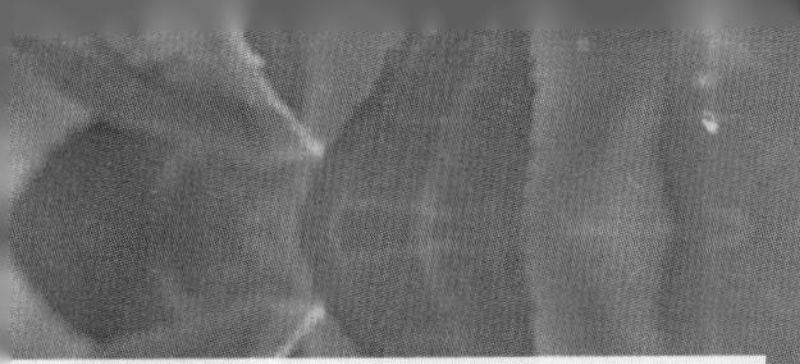

LENGTH: 3".

HABITAT: Weedy fresh water.

RANGE:

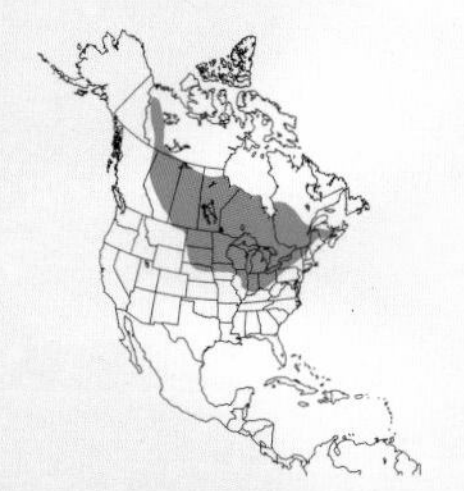

THREESPINE STICKLEBACK
Gasterosteus aculeatus

LOOK FOR: A greenish stickleback with 3 dorsal spines, the first 2 longer than the third. Marine varieties have plates along sides. **LENGTH:** 4". **HABITAT:** Fresh and salt water. **RANGE:** Alaska to Baja California, Mexico; Hudson Bay, Canada, to Virginia.

FOURSPINE STICKLEBACK
Apeltes quadracus

LOOK FOR: A brownish stickleback with 4 dorsal fin spines, the last attached to second dorsal fin. Males have red pelvic fins. **LENGTH:** 2". **HABITAT:** Salt and brackish water; freshwater estuaries. **RANGE:** Gulf of St. Lawrence, Canada, to North Carolina.

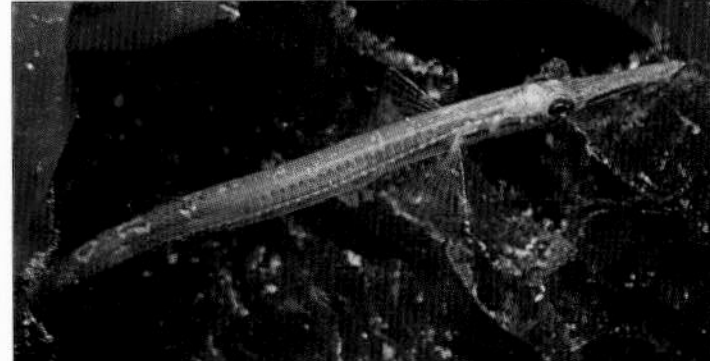

TUBE-SNOUT
Aulorhynchus flavidus

LOOK FOR: A very slender stickleback with a small mouth and long face. About 25 free spines in front of dorsal fin. **LENGTH:** 6". **HABITAT:** Saltwater kelp beds. **RANGE:** Alaska to Baja California, Mexico.

Northern Pipefish

Syngnathus fuscus

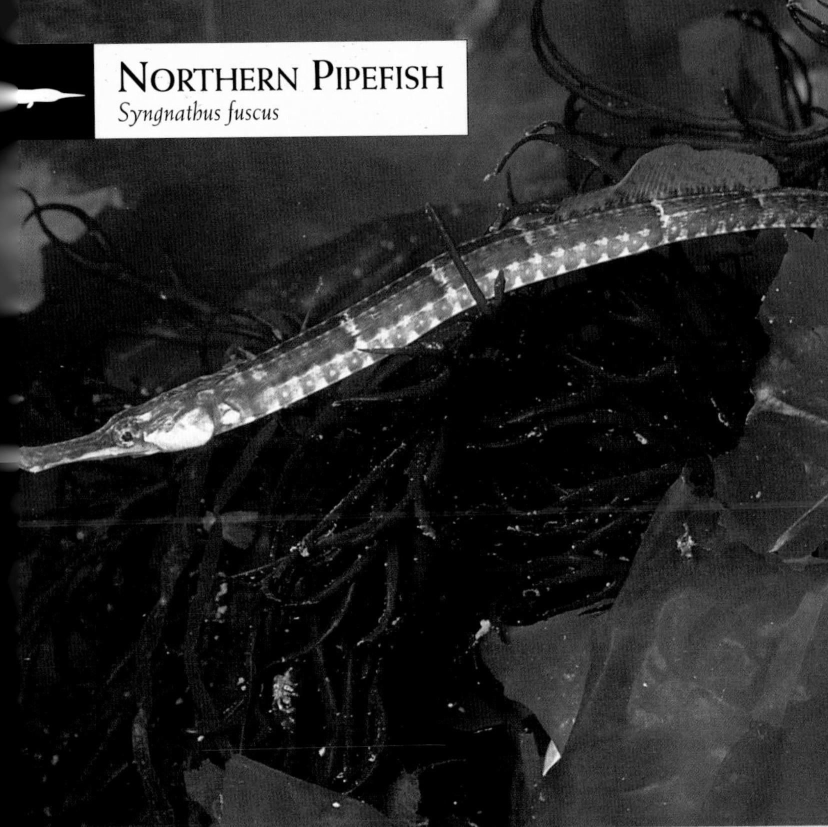

Pipefishes and seahorses are among the strangest-looking fishes in the ocean. Their bodies are encased in bony rings, and they have tiny mouths at the end of long faces. The Northern Pipefish, like the other fishes in this family, carries its eggs in special pouches on the lower part of the body until they hatch. The female deposits the eggs in the male's pouch, where they are fertilized and carried for roughly ten days. Seahorses are closely related to pipefishes, but instead of a tail fin, they have a fingerlike tail which they use to hold on to vegetation and other underwater surfaces.

Look for: A pipefish with a slender, stiff body encircled with bony rings. Small tail fin. Snout long and slender.

Length: 11".

Habitat: Salt or brackish water.

Range:

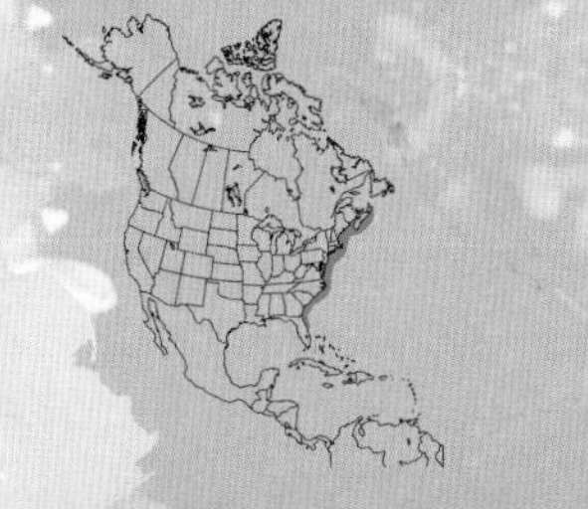

RELATED SPECIES

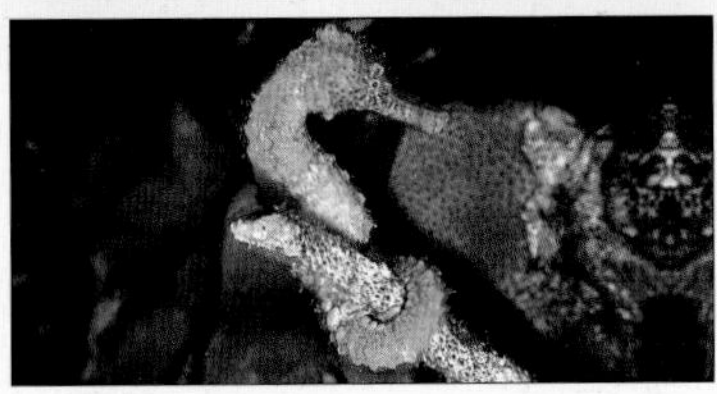

Lined Seahorse

Hippocampus erectus

Look for: A seahorse with a body shaped like a question mark. Fingerlike tail with no fin. **Length:** 7". **Habitat:** Coastal waters to depths of 250'. **Range:** Nova Scotia to South America.

Trumpetfish

Aulostomus maculatus

Look for: A very elongate fish with a tubular face. Short barbel on chin. Rough-scaled body; no membrane connecting dorsal spines. **Length:** 3'. **Habitat:** Coral reefs. **Range:** Tropical and subtropical Atlantic from Florida and Bermuda to Brazil.

Bluespotted Cornetfish

Fistularia tabacaria

Look for: An elongate fish with long tubular face. No barbels, scales, dorsal spines, or bony rings. Long, threadlike tail. **Length:** 6' (without tail). **Habitat:** Shallow marine waters, in sea grasses. **Range:** New England to Brazil, Bermuda.

Striped Bass

Morone saxatilis

Growing as long as six feet, the Striped Bass is the largest fish in the temperate bass family. It lives mostly in coastal marine waters, but swims into fresh water to spawn. It is such a popular sport fish that freshwater populations have been introduced into many reservoirs in North America. The temperate basses are a family of silvery, spiny-rayed fishes with two separate dorsal fins and moderately forked tails. Their bodies are generally compressed and deep. They have three spines in the anal fin, and their lateral line stops at the base of the tail fin.

Look for: A large, silvery-white bass with dark lines along the sides. Juveniles also have indistinct vertical bands.

LENGTH: 6'.

HABITAT: Ocean. Spawns in freshwater estuaries.

RANGE:

WHITE BASS
Morone chrysops

LOOK FOR: A rather rectangular bass with 2 dorsal fins. Silvery, with dark lines along sides. Feeds near the surface in schools. **LENGTH:** 16". **HABITAT:** Lakes, larger streams. **RANGE:** Native to central U.S. and Great Lakes drainages. Introduced elsewhere.

WHITE PERCH
Morone americana

LOOK FOR: A silvery bass without distinct lines. **LENGTH:** 19". **HABITAT:** Salt and fresh water. **RANGE:** Cape Breton Island, Canada, to South Carolina. Introduced elsewhere.

YELLOW BASS
Morone mississippiensis

LOOK FOR: A yellowish bass with stripes. **LENGTH:** 11". **HABITAT:** Lakes, reservoirs, larger streams. **RANGE:** Mississippi River drainages, Gulf coast streams to Texas. Introduced elsewhere.

Red Grouper

Epinephelus morio

The Red Grouper is a member of the large and diverse sea bass family. Many sea basses are hermaphrodites, which means they have both male and female reproductive features. Some produce both eggs and sperm, and others mature as females and later transform into males. The smaller sea basses are often very colorful. Groupers are large fishes with relatively small scales. They tend to have stout, elongate bodies that are moderately compressed. They are important as food in many tropical areas.

Look for: A rosy-reddish grouper with indistinct pale blotches. Membranes of dorsal fin not indented behind spines. Second dorsal fin spine the longest. Anal fin has 8–9 rays.

LENGTH: 3'.

HABITAT: Coastal waters to depths of 300'.

RANGE:

GAG GROUPER

Mycteroperca microlepis

LOOK FOR: A gray grouper with 10–12 rays in the anal fin. Irregular, darker spots on sides. **LENGTH:** 4'. **HABITAT:** Coastal waters at depths of 65–250' with rocky bottoms and coral reefs. Juveniles in sea grasses, estuaries. **RANGE:** North Carolina to Florida.

BLACK SEA BASS

Centropristis striata

LOOK FOR: A black bass with pale spots on scales. Filaments on dorsal spines. Tail rounded in juveniles; adult tail has 3 points. **LENGTH:** 24". **HABITAT:** Coastal waters with rocky bottoms. Juveniles in sea grasses. **RANGE:** Massachusetts to Florida.

KELP BASS

Paralabrax clathratus

LOOK FOR: An olive-brown bass with white blotches on back. Third, fourth, and fifth dorsal spines same length. **LENGTH:** 28". **HABITAT:** Coastal waters to depths of 150'. **RANGE:** Oregon to Baja California, Mexico.

Yellow Perch

Perca flavescens

The perches are a family of spiny-rayed freshwater fishes with two dorsal fins and one or two anal fin spines. Most perches are elongate, moderately compressed fishes. They can be found throughout North America and especially in the Northeast. Many are valued sport and food fishes. Some species, such as the Yellow Perch and the Walleye, have sawtoothlike edges on their cheekbones. The Yellow Perch lives in schools in deep water and moves into shallower water to feed at dawn and dusk.

Look for: A yellowish perch with vertical bars on sides. Pelvic fins orange or red.

Length: 12".

HABITAT: Quiet waters of lakes, ponds, streams.

RANGE:

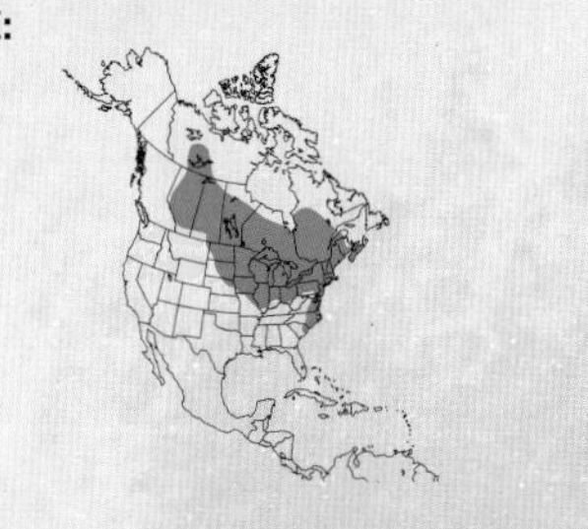

WALLEYE

Stizostedion vitreum

LOOK FOR: A large, elongate perch with indistinct diagonal bars on sides. Spot at base of last dorsal fin spines. **LENGTH:** 30". **HABITAT:** Lakes, slower parts of large streams. **RANGE:** Southeastern Canada, central and eastern U.S.

SAUGER

Stizostedion canadense

LOOK FOR: A perch similar to the Walleye but smaller and with rows of spots on first dorsal fin. No blotch at base of last dorsal spines. **LENGTH:** 20". **HABITAT:** Ponds, lakes, larger streams. **RANGE:** Canada, northern U.S.

RUFFE

Gymnocephalus cernuus

LOOK FOR: A small, greenish-brown perch with dark spots on back. Dorsal fin spines larger than soft rays. **LENGTH:** 10". **HABITAT:** Lakes, slow-moving streams. **RANGE:** Introduced from Europe into Great Lakes.

JOHNNY DARTER
Etheostoma nigrum

Despite their name, darters do not spend all their time darting around. Instead, they seem to be most content resting peacefully on the bottoms of quiet lakes and streams. Members of the perch family, they are small fishes with elongate bodies. There are about 150 species of darters, most of which live in freshwater streams. Many are extremely colorful. The Johnny Darter is a very widespread species. It lives well in captivity and is sometimes raised by scientists studying fish behavior.

LOOK FOR: A small, pale darter with tiny W-shaped markings on sides and nearly smooth cheekbones.

LENGTH: 3".

HABITAT: Lakes, ponds, quiet parts of streams.

RANGE:

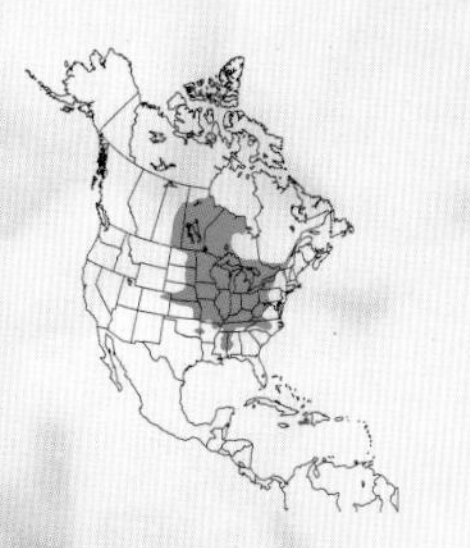

VARIEGATE DARTER

Etheostoma variatum

LOOK FOR: A medium-size darter with a broad, orange stripe along lower side. First dorsal fin has red band near edge and blue-black band in center. **LENGTH:** 4". **HABITAT:** Moderately swift streams. **RANGE:** Ohio River drainages.

LOGPERCH

Percina caprodes

LOOK FOR: A large darter with an overhanging conical snout. Pale yellow with alternating long and short vertical bars. **LENGTH:** 6". **HABITAT:** Lakes, rivers, small streams. **RANGE:** South-central Canada, central U.S.

SNAIL DARTER

Percina tanasi

LOOK FOR: A brown darter with 4 dark brown, saddle-shaped marks and dark stripe along sides. **LENGTH:** 3½". **HABITAT:** Gravel and sand shallows. **RANGE:** Lower Tennessee River.

Largemouth Bass

Micropterus salmoides

Largemouth Basses love to clamp their large mouths down on other fishes, and anglers often go after this popular catch with live bait. They belong to the sunfish and bass family, Centrarchidae. Centrarchids are native to warm freshwater areas of North America and have been introduced throughout much of the continent. They are compressed, oval-shaped, spiny-rayed fishes with a continuous dorsal fin. Most live in lakes and streams, where their round, pebbly nests are a common sight in spring and summer.

Look for: A greenish bass with a broad stripe along the side that becomes more solid and continuous at the base of the tail. Dorsal fin deeply notched. Mouth extends behind eye in large fishes.

LENGTH: 27".

HABITAT: Weedy parts of lakes, ponds, streams.

RANGE:

SMALLMOUTH BASS

Micropterus dolomieu

LOOK FOR: A bronze bass with vertical bands. Small notches in dorsal fin. Juveniles have prominent bars and tricolor tail. **LENGTH:** 27". **HABITAT:** Lakes, streams; prefers rock and gravel bottoms. **RANGE:** Southern Canada, north-central U.S. Introduced elsewhere.

WARMOUTH

Lepomis gulosus

LOOK FOR: A heavy-bodied, compressed sunfish with 3 anal spines. Mottled brown with 4 dark bars across cheek. **LENGTH:** 11". **HABITAT:** Lakes, ponds, slower parts of streams. **RANGE:** Central and southern U.S.

GREEN SUNFISH

Lepomis cyanellus

LOOK FOR: A greenish sunfish with a large mouth and short, rounded pectoral fins. Yellow or orange belly. Dark spot at back of dorsal fin. **LENGTH:** 10". **HABITAT:** Lakes, ponds, slow-moving streams. **RANGE:** Native to central U.S. Introduced elsewhere.

Rock Bass

Ambloplites rupestris

One of the outstanding features of the Rock Bass is its size: It fits perfectly in a frying pan. This "panfish" is popular among anglers, as are many of its smaller relatives in the freshwater sunfish and bass family (Centrarchidae). Like its relatives, the Rock Bass is a spiny-rayed fish with a continuous dorsal fin and a heavy, compressed body. It also has a large head and a wide mouth.

Look for: A heavy-bodied, compressed sunfish with 5 anal fin spines. Brownish or brassy with dark streaks. Adults have red eyes. Juveniles have dark and light squarish blotches on sides.

Length: 9".

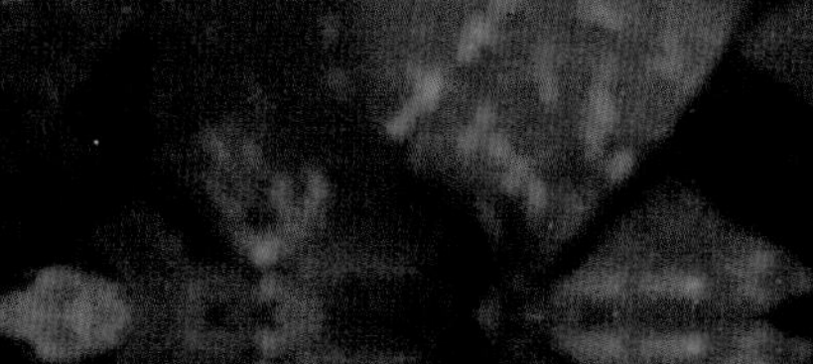

Habitat: Lakes, ponds, streams.

Range:

RELATED SPECIES

White Crappie

Pomoxis annularis

Look for: A silvery-green, diamond-shaped sunfish with irregular vertical bars. Short, high dorsal fin with 6–7 spines. **Length:** 13". **Habitat:** Lakes, slow-moving streams. **Range:** Central U.S., Mississippi River, Great Lakes drainages. Widely introduced.

Flier

Centrarchus macropterus

Look for: A greenish sunfish with spots. 7–8 anal spines. Dark bar below eye. Yellow-ringed black spot on juveniles' dorsal fin. **Length:** 7". **Habitat:** Swamps, slow-moving waters. **Range:** Illinois to Gulf of Mexico coast, Atlantic drainages to Virginia.

Sacramento Perch

Archoplites interruptus

Look for: A sunfish with 6–7 anal spines and 12–13 dorsal spines. Back dark brown with about 7 vertical dark bars. **Length:** 24". **Habitat:** Ponds, reservoirs. **Range:** Native to Central Valley, California. Introduced in Nevada and elsewhere.

BLUEGILL

Lepomis macrochirus

The Bluegill has the unenviable distinction of being stocked to serve as food for larger fishes. Widely distributed, this excellent sport and food fish is popular throughout its range as a panfish (a small fish that is easily caught and fried whole in a pan). It is a member of the spiny-rayed sunfish and bass family (Centrarchidae) and has a continuous dorsal fin and a heavy, oval-shaped body that is very compressed.

LOOK FOR: A small sunfish with a deep, compressed body. Dark spot on back of dorsal fin. Black, flexible flap on gill cover.

LENGTH: 13".

HABITAT: Lakes, ponds, slower parts of freshwater streams.

RANGE:

PUMPKINSEED

Lepomis gibbosus

LOOK FOR: A heavy-bodied sunfish with white edge and red spot on gill flap. **LENGTH:** 16". **HABITAT:** Lakes, ponds, slower parts of streams. **RANGE:** Great Lakes drainages, upper Mississippi River, and northern Atlantic coast.

ORANGESPOTTED SUNFISH

Lepomis humilis

LOOK FOR: A small, oval-shaped sunfish with white edge on gill flap. Orange-red spots on sides. **LENGTH:** 4". **HABITAT:** Quiet waters. **RANGE:** Mississippi River drainages. Introduced in southern Great Lakes.

LONGEAR SUNFISH

Lepomis megalotis

LOOK FOR: A deep-bodied sunfish with a short, rounded pectoral fin. Gill flap long with pale edge in northern populations. **LENGTH:** 10". **HABITAT:** Quiet waters. **RANGE:** Great Lakes, central North America from southern Ontario to Texas.

Freshwater Drum

Aplodinotus grunniens

Have you ever heard a funny noise while out fish-watching? It might well have been a drum. These fishes get their name from their ability to make a drumming or croaking noise by using special muscles attached to the swim bladder. With the exception of the Freshwater Drum, these fish live in salt water. Drums have two anal fin spines and two dorsal fins—one short and spiny, the other long and soft. Their scales are rough, and the lateral line continues to the end of the tail. The Freshwater Drum has the widest north-to-south range of any freshwater fish in North America.

Look for: A moderately large, silvery-gray drum. Males have yellow pelvic fins with first ray short and threadlike. Mouth low

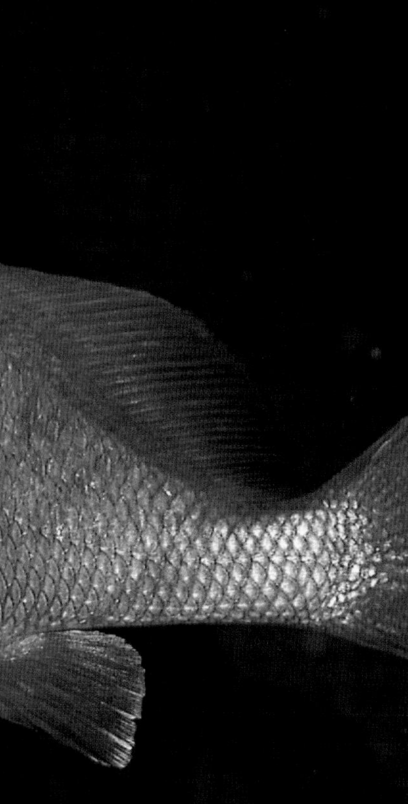

and horizontal; overhanging snout.

LENGTH: 3'.

HABITAT: Lakes, large rivers.

RANGE:

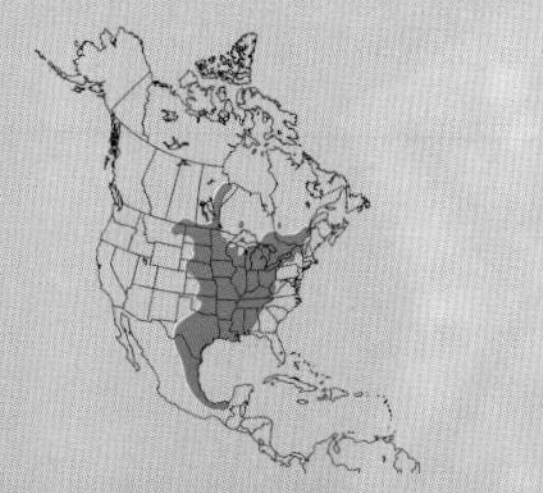

ATLANTIC CROAKER

Micropogonias undulatus

LOOK FOR: A drum with a low, horizontal mouth and 3–5 pairs of short barbels on chin. Silvery-gray above with numerous spots forming slanted bars. **LENGTH:** 18". **HABITAT:** Coastal waters, estuaries. **RANGE:** Massachusetts to Florida, Gulf of Mexico.

SPOTTED SEATROUT

Cynoscion nebulosus

LOOK FOR: An elongate, silvery-gray drum. Black spots on back and on dorsal and tail fins. 2 large, fanglike teeth on upper jaw. **LENGTH:** 3'. **HABITAT:** Shallow, sandy-bottomed coastal waters near sea grasses. **RANGE:** Cape Cod, Massachusetts, to Gulf of Mexico.

SILVER PERCH

Bairdiella chrysoura

LOOK FOR: A silvery-gray drum without distinct markings. No barbels on chin. **LENGTH:** 12". **HABITAT:** Coastal waters, lower parts of estuaries. **RANGE:** New York to northern Mexico.

Gray Snapper

Lutjanus griseus

Gray Snappers often swim and feed together in large schools. They are predatory and use their sharp teeth to catch smaller fishes. Their spawning period is in the summer, usually around the full moon. Snappers are elongate fishes with deep, compressed bodies and a continuous dorsal fin. They are important game and food fishes.

Look for: A grayish snapper with a dark stripe from snout through eye to upper end of gill openings. The edge of the dorsal fin is black; square tail fin.

Length: 24".

HABITAT: Coastal areas; around mangroves in warmer parts of range.

RANGE:

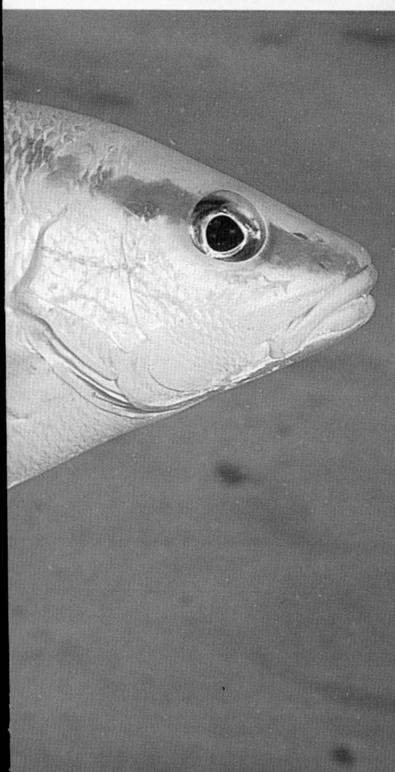

RELATED SPECIES

GLASSEYE SNAPPER
Heteropriacanthus cruentatus

LOOK FOR: A red, compressed, deep-bodied fish. Large eyes (to see in dark), rough scales, and square tail. Member of bigeye family. **LENGTH:** 10". **HABITAT:** Warm coral reefs, saltwater caves, under overhangs. **RANGE:** Pacific and Atlantic coasts.

YELLOWTAIL SNAPPER
Ocyurus chrysurus

LOOK FOR: A graceful snapper with a forked tail. Yellow stripe on sides extends to both parts of tail fin. **LENGTH:** 28". **HABITAT:** Coral reefs, inshore habitats. **RANGE:** Massachusetts to Brazil, including West Indies.

FLAMEFISH
Apogon maculatus

LOOK FOR: A small, red fish with a black spot on upper side below second dorsal fin and a dark band at base of tail. Big eyes marked with 2 white lines. **LENGTH:** 2¾". **HABITAT:** Coral reefs, caves, to depths of 400'. **RANGE:** New England to northern South America, including West Indies.

SHEEPSHEAD

Archosargus probatocephalus

Like many other porgies, the Sheepshead has broad, flat teeth in the front of its mouth and wide molars on the sides of its jaws. It uses its teeth to grind up small crabs and to scrape barnacles off underwater ledges. Porgies are saltwater fishes characterized by a single dorsal fin and forked tail. They generally have deep, oval, compressed bodies and large heads.

LOOK FOR: A grayish porgy with 6 broad, dark vertical bars.

LENGTH: 3'.

HABITAT: Shallow coastal waters; sometimes in lower parts of estuaries.

RANGE:

JOLTHEAD PORGY

Calamus bajonado

LOOK FOR: A silvery-blue porgy with a blue line under each eye. Back highly arched. **LENGTH:** 27". **HABITAT:** Sand and coral ocean bottoms to depths of 660'. **RANGE:** Carolinas to Brazil, eastern Gulf of Mexico.

PINFISH

Lagodon rhomboides

LOOK FOR: A silvery porgy with yellow lines on sides. Spot on "shoulder" centered on lateral line. 4–6 indistinct vertical dark bars. **LENGTH:** 15". **HABITAT:** Shallow coastal waters with vegetation. **RANGE:** Massachusetts to Florida, north coast of Cuba.

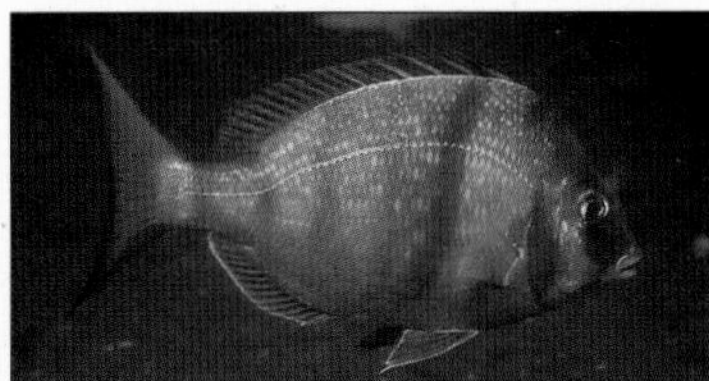

SCUP

Stenotomus chrysops

LOOK FOR: A bluish-silvery porgy with 6–7 faint bars on upper sides. **LENGTH:** 12". **HABITAT:** Coastal waters with rocky bottoms and man-made structures; deeper waters in winter. **RANGE:** Nova Scotia to eastern Florida.

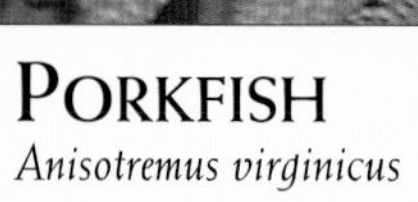

Porkfish

Anisotremus virginicus

Your ears will help you identify this fish. A member of the grunt family, the Porkfish can produce a peculiar grunting sound by rubbing together the teeth in its throat. If their grunting puts you off, you may still be charmed by the characteristic "smiling" expression grunts have when their mouths are closed. When open, their mouths show a bright red lining, which they often display to each other in territorial contests. Grunts are a group of small to midsize basslike fishes that have deep, compressed, oval-shaped bodies.

Look for: A small, silvery grunt with prominent, yellow fins and side stripes and 2 broad, black vertical bars, one through the eye and one behind the head.

LENGTH: 15".

HABITAT: Coral reefs, mangroves, grassy coastal waters.

RANGE:

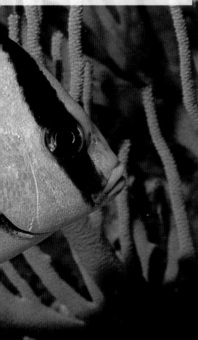

FRENCH GRUNT

Haemulon flavolineatum

LOOK FOR: A bluish grunt with horizontal yellow lines that slope upward below lateral line. Scales larger below lateral line than above. **LENGTH:** 9". **HABITAT:** Coral reefs and sea grasses to depths of 80'. **RANGE:** Southern Florida to Brazil.

WHITE GRUNT

Haemulon plumieri

LOOK FOR: A midsize grunt with narrow, blue stripes on sides of head. Scales larger above lateral line. Often with broad dark stripe on front half of side. **LENGTH:** 17". **HABITAT:** Reefs, sea-grass beds. **RANGE:** Maryland to Brazil, including West Indies.

YELLOWFIN MOJARRA

Gerres cinereus

LOOK FOR: A deep, compressed fish with 7–8 short, thin vertical bars along sides. Pelvic and anal fins yellow. **LENGTH:** 15". **HABITAT:** Reefs, sea-grass beds. **RANGE:** Florida to Brazil, eastern Pacific.

CREVALLE JACK

Caranx hippos

Like grunts, Crevalle Jacks are able to produce a grunting or croaking sound. Smaller Crevalle Jacks travel together in schools, but they prefer solitude as they get larger. Jacks are a large family of graceful, silvery fishes with deeply forked tails. They tend to have very compressed, deep, spindle-shaped bodies. They often have platelike scutes along some or all of the lateral line.

LOOK FOR: A large, silvery jack with a large, dark spot on upper margin of gill cover. Dark spot on pectoral fin.

LENGTH: 3'.

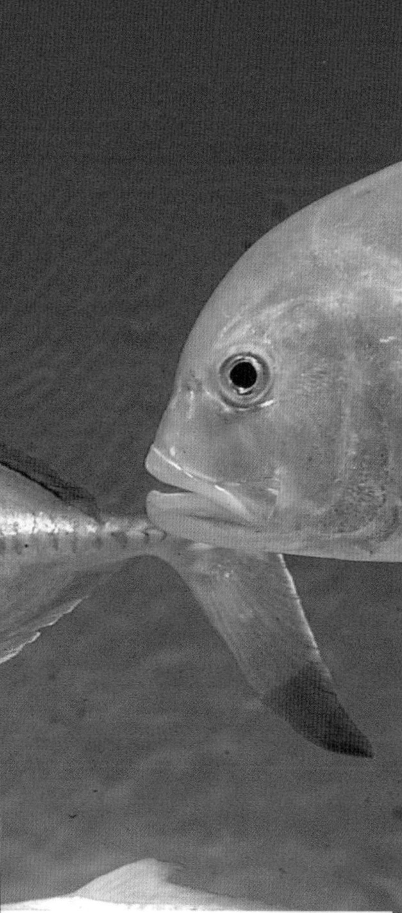

HABITAT: Shallow coastal areas. Juveniles in estuaries.

RANGE:

RELATED SPECIES

BAR JACK
Caranx ruber

LOOK FOR: A slender jack with darker color of back extending downward onto lower lobe of tail fin. **LENGTH:** 16". **HABITAT:** Clear shallow coastal waters; coral reefs. **RANGE:** New Jersey to Venezuela, West Indies.

YELLOWTAIL
Seriola lalandei

LOOK FOR: A large, sleek jack without scutes on base of tail fin. Gray above with yellow stripe on mid-side. **LENGTH:** 5'. **HABITAT:** Coastal waters to depths of 80'. **RANGE:** Washington state to Chile.

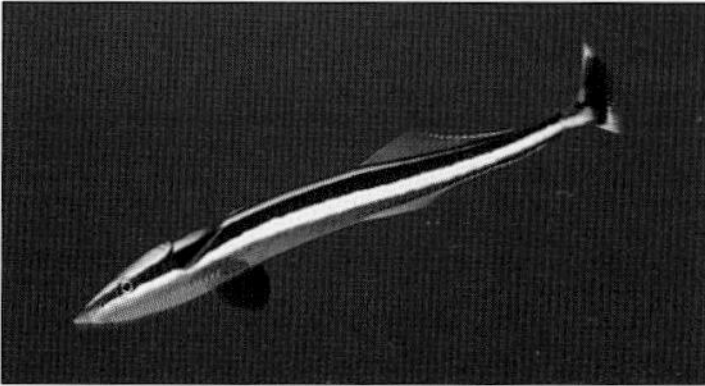

SHARKSUCKER
Echeneis naucrates

LOOK FOR: A slender fish with black and white stripes. Suckerlike disk on top of head with plates that resemble window blinds. Attaches to other fishes using sucking disk. **LENGTH:** 3'. **HABITAT:** Warm open seas. **RANGE:** Pacific and Atlantic oceans.

FOUREYE BUTTERFLYFISH
Chaetodon capistratus

If you see a butterflyfish alone, chances are it is looking for its partner. With the exception of a few loner species, most of these fishes pair off early and will search for each other when they get separated. Butterflies and their relatives, the angelfishes, are among the most colorful fishes you can see in coral reefs. Both families are deep-bodied, disk-shaped fishes that look quite similar, except that angelfishes have large spines on their cheekbones.

LOOK FOR: A large, disk-shaped butterflyfish with a black spot surrounded by a white ring located below rear of dorsal fin. Narrow lines on sides forming Vs.

LENGTH: 3".

HABITAT: Coral reefs and other inshore habitats.

RANGE:

GRAY ANGELFISH

Pomacanthus arcuatus

LOOK FOR: A large, grayish-brown, marbled-looking angelfish with light margins on scales. Large spine on cheekbone. Juveniles black with narrow, yellow vertical bars. **LENGTH:** 14". **HABITAT:** Coral reefs. **RANGE:** New England to Brazil, including West Indies.

QUEEN ANGELFISH

Holacanthus ciliaris

LOOK FOR: A large, blue angelfish with yellow tail and round, black spot on forehead. Spot ringed in blue and peppered with small blue spots. **LENGTH:** 12". **HABITAT:** Coral reefs. **RANGE:** Florida to South America, including West Indies.

CHERUBFISH

Centropyge argi

LOOK FOR: A small, blue angelfish with an orange face, chest, and pectoral fin. Blue ring around eye. Large spine on cheekbone. **LENGTH:** 2". **HABITAT:** Coral reefs. **RANGE:** Bermuda, Florida to northern South America.

SERGEANT MAJOR
Abudefduf saxatilis

The Sergeant Major not only wears a "uniform" (the dark bars on its side look like military insignia, hence its name), but also guards its feeding territories vigorously and will attack any intruders, including snorkelers. It is quite harmless, however—it is too small and its teeth are too blunt to hurt you. In the breeding period, Sergeant Major males turn blue while they are guarding their eggs. The Sergeant Major is one of the damselfishes, a family of small, compressed, deep-bodied fishes that are very common on coral reefs. Most damselfishes guard their eggs fiercely.

LOOK FOR: A deep-bodied, compressed damselfish. Yellow, with 5 vertical black bars.

LENGTH: To 8".

HABITAT: Coral reefs and associated habitats; often inshore around rocks and man-made structures.

RANGE:

BEAUGREGORY

Stegastes leucostictus

LOOK FOR: A small, plain damselfish, blue above and yellow below. Dark spot near back of dorsal fin. **LENGTH:** 4". **HABITAT:** Around mangroves, coastal waters with vegetation, coral reefs. **RANGE:** Atlantic coast to Brazil, Bermuda, West Indies.

BLACKSMITH

Chromis punctipinnis

LOOK FOR: A dark, blue-gray damselfish. Small, black spots on dorsal fin and rear half of body. **LENGTH:** 12". **HABITAT:** Kelp beds, coastal waters to depths of 150'. **RANGE:** Monterey Bay, California, to Baja California, Mexico.

GARIBALDI

Hypsypops rubicundus

LOOK FOR: A chubby, bright reddish-orange damselfish. **LENGTH:** 14". **HABITAT:** Kelp beds, coastal waters to depths of 95'. **RANGE:** Monterey Bay, California, to Baja California, Mexico.

Tautog

Tautoga onitis

The Tautog has a blunt snout and thick, fleshy lips that cover its strong, conical teeth. It uses these teeth to crush its favorite food: shellfish from the ocean bottom. The Tautog is a member of the wrasse family. Like the other wrasses, it has a single dorsal fin with weak spines. Wrasses have compressed bodies and range in shape from elongate to deep. Most wrasses are abundant around coral reefs, but the Tautog is one of a few species that prefers cooler, temperate waters.

Look for: A compressed, black or gray wrasse with a dark, marbled pattern. Cheeks scaleless. Mature males black with white chin.

Length: 3'.

HABITAT: Juveniles in sea-grass beds; adults around rocks and man-made structures.

RANGE:

BLUEHEAD
Thalassoma bifasciatum

LOOK FOR: A yellow wrasse with broad, reddish-brown stripe on side. Older males (supermales) greenish with blue head, 2 black bands and sky-blue patch at front of body. **LENGTH:** 5". **HABITAT:** Coral reefs. **RANGE:** Florida to South America, West Indies.

SLIPPERY DICK
Halichoeres bivittatus

LOOK FOR: A large, greenish-gray wrasse with 2 narrow, dark stripes along sides. Black tips on tail fin lobes. **LENGTH:** 7". **HABITAT:** Coral reefs, sea-grass beds, mangrove shorelines. **RANGE:** Florida to northern South America, Bermuda, West Indies.

HOGFISH
Lachnolaimus maximus

LOOK FOR: A large wrasse with large, pointed head. First 3 dorsal spines very long. **LENGTH:** 3'. **HABITAT:** Coral reefs, shallow shorelines. **RANGE:** Canada to northern South America, Bermuda, West Indies.

Queen Parrotfish

Scarus vetula

YOUNG ADULT

As parrotfishes grow up, they don't just get bigger, they also change color and sometimes transform from females into males. They have deep, compressed bodies, and their teeth are fused into beaklike plates. The Queen Parrotfish has two distinct color patterns. Young adults are gray with a broad, white side stripe. Certain older males, known as supermales, are blue-green. Queen Parrotfish of all ages swim together in schools and feed on algae growing on coral and limestone rock.

LOOK FOR: A deep-bodied, gray fish with a broad, white side stripe. Supermales are blue-green and have a brownish-orange stripe on the upper edge of the pectoral fin.

LENGTH: 20".

HABITAT: Coral reefs.

RANGE:

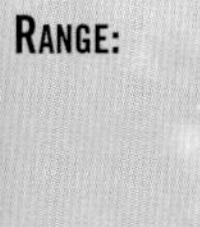

STRIPED PARROTFISH
Scarus iserti

LOOK FOR: A blue-green parrotfish, often with yellow on top of head (supermales). Females and juveniles gray with white stripes. Upper stripe ends at eye. **LENGTH:** 11". **HABITAT:** Coral reefs. **RANGE:** Florida to Brazil, Bermuda, West Indies.

STOPLIGHT PARROTFISH
Sparisoma viride

LOOK FOR: A green parrotfish with yellow spot at top of gill cover, yellow crescents at tail base (supermales). Female (pictured) gray and black with bright red belly. **LENGTH:** 22". **HABITAT:** Coral reefs. **RANGE:** Florida to Brazil, Bermuda, West Indies.

RAINBOW PARROTFISH
Scarus guacamaia

LOOK FOR: A large, red-brown and green parrotfish with green teeth. **LENGTH:** 4'. **HABITAT:** Rocky and mangrove shorelines, coral reefs. **RANGE:** Florida to Argentina, West Indies.

Sailfin Blenny

Emblemaria pandionis

When they are ready to breed, male Sailfin Blennies set up shelter in a hole in the coral reef and then flap their large dorsal fins in an effort to attract egg-laying females. There are three related families called blennies: pikeblennies, labrisomids, and combtooth blennies. All are elongate fishes with the pelvic fins far forward and with two or three visible rays. Most blennies have fleshy fingerlike tentacles (called cirri) on the eye, nostrils, and back of the head. Pikeblennies are scaleless and have conical teeth. Labrisomids have scales and bushy cirri on the back of the head and over the eyes. Combtooth blennies are also scaleless and have blunt heads and very fine teeth.

Look for: A pikeblenny with very large dorsal fin. Males black in

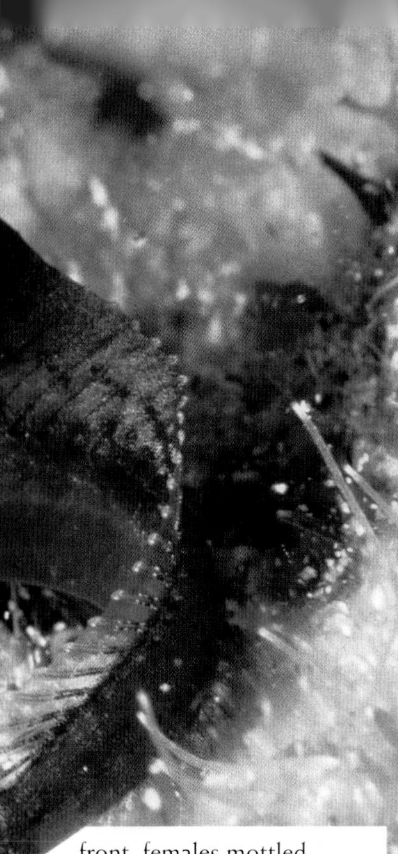

front, females mottled.

LENGTH: 2".

HABITAT: Coral reefs in sandy areas.

RANGE:

HAIRY BLENNY
Labrisomus nuchipinnis

LOOK FOR: A large, greenish-yellow labrisomid with a dark spot ringed in white on gill cover. **LENGTH:** 7". **HABITAT:** Coral reefs and other rocky areas. **RANGE:** Florida to Brazil, Bermuda, West Indies.

REDLIP BLENNY
Ophioblennius atlanticus

LOOK FOR: An elongate combtooth blenny with a brown head and red lips. **LENGTH:** $4\frac{1}{2}$". **HABITAT:** Rocky shorelines. **RANGE:** Florida to Brazil, Bermuda, West Indies.

MOLLY MILLER
Scartella cristata

LOOK FOR: An elongate, greenish-gray combtooth blenny with a row of cirri on head. **LENGTH:** 4". **HABITAT:** Rocky shorelines, tide pools. **RANGE:** Florida to Brazil, West Indies.

NEON GOBY

Gobiosoma oceanops

The Neon Goby acts like a kind of "cleaner fish," eating parasites and other material off the bodies of other fishes. It belongs to a family of small, elongate, predominantly saltwater fishes. There are more kinds of gobies than there are of any other family of saltwater fishes. There are also a few freshwater species of gobies found in estuaries and lakes. On most gobies, the pelvic fins are fused to form a suckerlike disk, but some have separate pelvic fins. Gobies spend much of their time hiding or resting motionless on the bottom.

LOOK FOR: A dark goby without scales. Black above and pale below with electric-blue stripe on upper side and black stripe on mid-side.

LENGTH: 1".

HABITAT: Living coral reefs, in presence of other fishes.

RANGE:

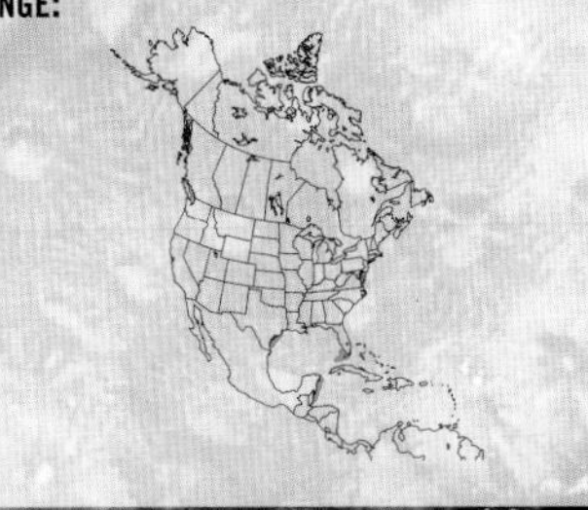

FRILLFIN GOBY

Bathygobius soporator

LOOK FOR: A yellowish-brown goby with the upper rays of the pectoral fin free (not connected by membrane). **LENGTH:** 6". **HABITAT:** Tide pools, rocky shorelines. **RANGE:** North Carolina to Brazil, Bermuda, West Indies.

FRESHWATER GOBY

Gobionellus shufeldti

LOOK FOR: A pale tan goby with 5 dark blotches along sides. **LENGTH:** 3". **HABITAT:** Estuaries; enters freshwater rivers. **RANGE:** North Carolina to Florida, northern Gulf of Mexico near Mississippi delta.

ROUND GOBY

Neogobius melanostomus

LOOK FOR: A grayish-brown goby with spot on spiny dorsal fin. **LENGTH:** 12". **HABITAT:** Around rocks and other shelter; abundant in colonies of zebra mussels. **RANGE:** Native to Caspian and Black seas; introduced into western Lake Erie.

SAILFISH
Istiophorus platypterus

The Sailfish has a huge, sail-like dorsal fin that sometimes sticks out of the water as it glides along near the ocean surface. This fin can be as much as two times as high as the Sailfish's body. As a member of the billfish family, the Sailfish has a long snout that extends into an even longer spikelike "bill." Billfishes are strong, elongate, compressed game fishes that will fight for hours if caught by an offshore angler. The Sailfish is shaded dark blue above with rows of pale blue spots. Its belly is almost white.

LOOK FOR: A slender, long billfish with a sail-like dorsal fin and a sharp, pointed snout.

LENGTH: 8'.

HABITAT: Warm open ocean waters; near surface.

RANGE:

GREAT BARRACUDA
Sphyraena barracuda

LOOK FOR: A slender fish with 2 dorsal fins and a large mouth. Gray above; silvery sides. Dark spots above anal fin. **LENGTH:** 6'. **HABITAT:** Warm coastal waters, open ocean. Juveniles often near shore. **RANGE:** Pacific and Atlantic coasts. **CAUTION:** Known to attack swimmers.

YELLOWFIN TUNA
Thunnus albacares

LOOK FOR: A spindle-shaped fish with high second dorsal and anal fins; small yellow "finlets" along top length. Popular food fish. **LENGTH:** 7'. **HABITAT:** Warm open ocean waters; near surface. **RANGE:** Pacific and Atlantic oceans.

ATLANTIC MACKEREL
Scomber scombrus

LOOK FOR: A slender, spindle-shaped fish with 2 well-separated dorsal fins and wavy dark lines across blue back. **LENGTH:** 20". **HABITAT:** Coastal waters, open ocean. **RANGE:** Labrador to North Carolina.

Mottled Sculpin

Cottus bairdi

Sculpins are timid fish that can often be seen in shallow areas near stones, under which they hide if they feel threatened. They live in freshwater streams and feed mainly on insect larvae. Sculpins are small, elongate, scaleless fishes with two dorsal fins and very large pectoral fins. Their heads are broad and flat, with large mouths. They have three or four rays in the pelvic fins.

Look for: A sculpin with 2 dorsal fins joined at base and 2 dark spots on each dorsal fin. 4 pelvic fin rays.

Length: 5".

HABITAT: Streams with gravel bottoms.

RANGE:

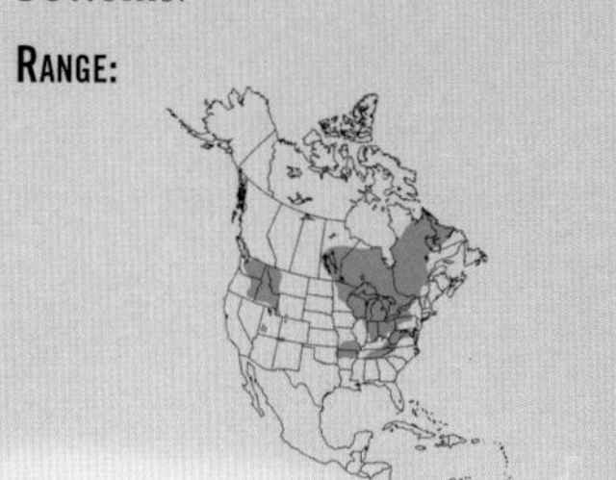

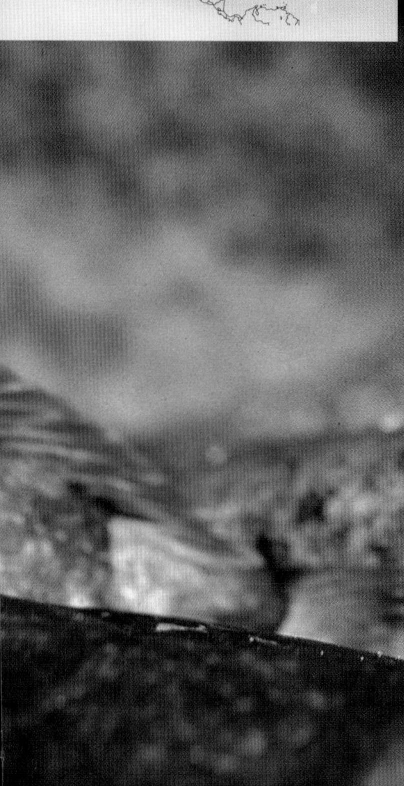

SEA RAVEN

Hemitripterus americanus

LOOK FOR: A sculpin with prickly skin. 3 long dorsal spines. Membrane of first dorsal fin deeply notched between spines. Fleshy tabs on head. **LENGTH:** 25". **HABITAT:** Ocean bottoms at depths of 10–200'. **RANGE:** Labrador to Chesapeake Bay.

CABEZON

Scorpaenichthys marmoratus

LOOK FOR: A sculpin with a fleshy tab on midline of snout. **LENGTH:** 3'3". **HABITAT:** Coastlines to depths of 250'. **RANGE:** Alaska to southern California.

STRIPED SEAROBIN

Prionotus evolans

LOOK FOR: A slender fish with a large head. Narrow, black stripes on sides. Large, brown pectoral fin with narrow, dusky stripes. **LENGTH:** 18". **HABITAT:** Sandy ocean bottoms to depths of 500'. **RANGE:** Nova Scotia to Florida.

Hogchoker

Trinectus maculatus

It is said that Hogchokers were once so common that they were used as food for pigs. Occasionally one would get stuck in a hog's throat, giving this fish its common name. The Hogchoker is a flatfish, a group of extremely flat-bodied fishes that live on ocean and stream bottoms. Flatfishes have both eyes on one side of their bodies (the right or the left). They swim on their sides with both eyes pointing up, so they can keep watch overhead. The eyed side has a color pattern, while the blind side is usually nearly white. These fishes can rapidly nestle down and blend in with their surroundings. The Hogchoker is an American sole, a family of small, round, righteye flatfishes.

Look for: A round sole with eyes on the right side.

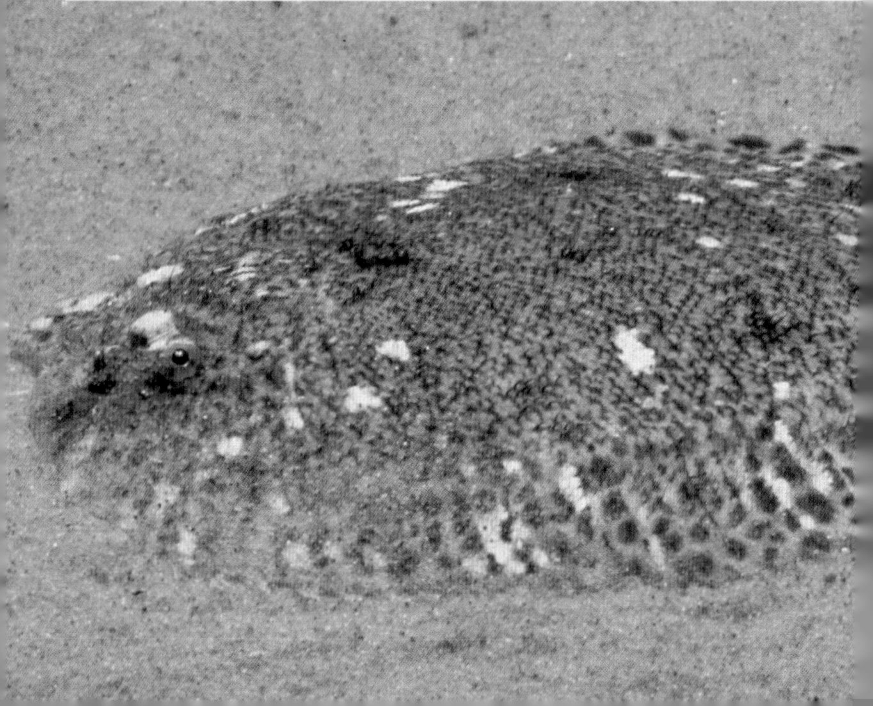

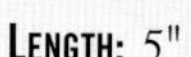

LENGTH: 5".

HABITAT: Sandy bottoms of coastal shorelines and estuaries. Also found in freshwater far upstream.

RANGE:

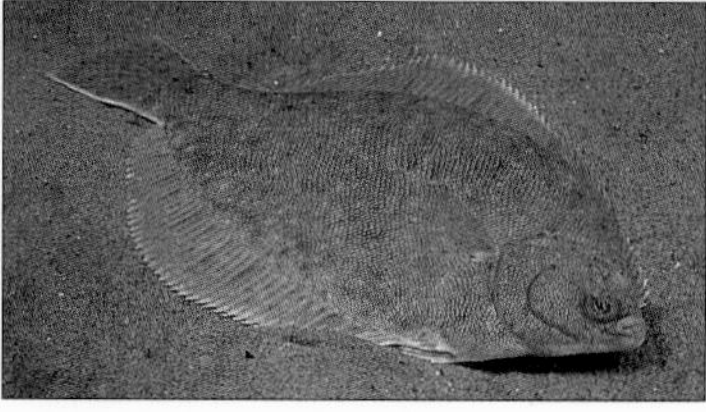

WINTER FLOUNDER

Pleuronectes americanus

LOOK FOR: A small-mouthed, righteye flatfish. Important food fish. **LENGTH:** 25". **HABITAT:** Sandy bottoms of coastal shorelines and estuaries. **RANGE:** Southern Labrador to Georgia.

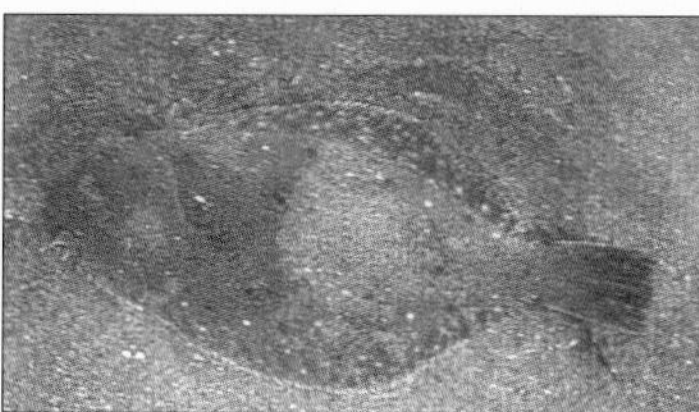

ATLANTIC HALIBUT

Hippoglossus hippoglossus

LOOK FOR: A huge, righteye flatfish. **LENGTH:** 6'. **HABITAT:** Sand, gravel, or clay ocean bottoms at depths of 200–3,000'. **RANGE:** Greenland to New Jersey.

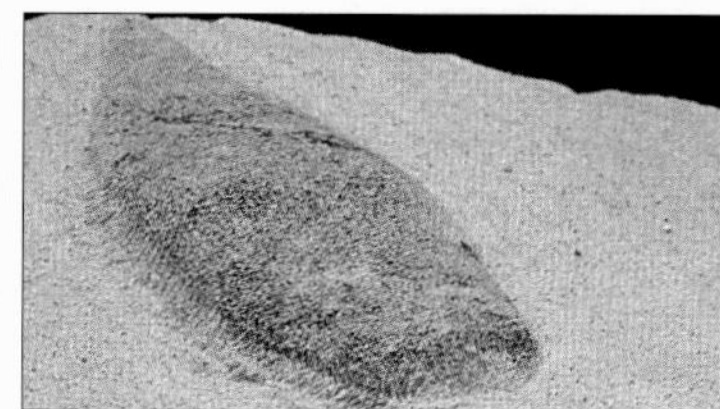

BLACKCHEEK TONGUEFISH

Symphurus plagiusa

LOOK FOR: A tongue-shaped, lefteye flatfish. Dorsal and anal fins joined to the tail. **LENGTH:** 7". **HABITAT:** Muddy bottoms of coastal waters. **RANGE:** New York to Gulf of Mexico, West Indies.

BLUE TANG
Acanthurus coeruleus
JUVENILE

The ocean is full of hungry predators, and the fishes in the four families shown here have all developed a defensive weapon on their bodies. Triggerfishes and filefishes both have a very sharp first dorsal spine. Boxfishes have platelike scales that form a stiff, protective armor—like a box—around their entire bodies. Surgeonfishes have two scalpel-like spines on their underside (at the base of the tail fin) that can be extended as a kind of spike. Like the other surgeonfishes, the pretty Blue Tang is among the most noticeable fishes on coral reefs. It is usually bright yellow when young and generally becomes bright blue as an adult.

LOOK FOR: A compressed, deep-bodied, almost disk-shaped blue surgeonfish with yellow spines on the base of the tail fin.

LENGTH: 14".

HABITAT: Coral reefs.

RANGE:

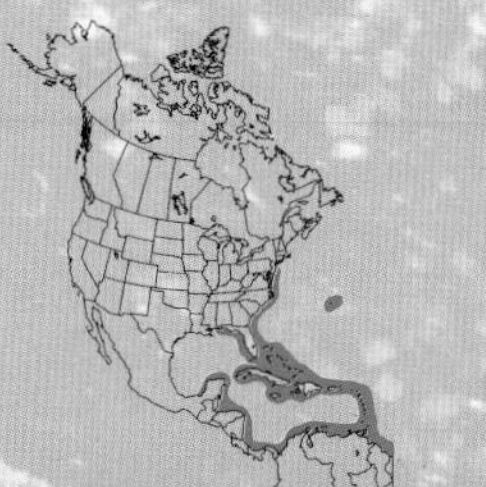

RELATED SPECIES

GRAY TRIGGERFISH

Balistes capriscus

LOOK FOR: A large triggerfish with hard scales. First dorsal fin has 3 spines, second spine (or "trigger") locks first one in upright position. **LENGTH:** 16". **HABITAT:** Ocean bottoms and coral reefs to depths of 165'. **RANGE:** Nova Scotia to Argentina, West Indies.

SCRAWLED FILEFISH

Aluterus scriptus

LOOK FOR: A compressed, yellowish-tan filefish with blue lines and spots. Spiky first dorsal spine. Tail very long. **LENGTH:** 3'. **HABITAT:** Open waters, coral reefs, sea-grass beds. **RANGE:** Nova Scotia to Brazil.

SCRAWLED COWFISH

Lactophrys quadricornis

LOOK FOR: A brownish, deep-bodied boxfish with numerous blue lines and spots. Triangular in cross section. Bony "cow horns" on head. **LENGTH:** 14". **HABITAT:** Sea-grass beds to depths of 265'. **RANGE:** Massachusetts to Brazil, Bermuda.

Northern Puffer

Sphoeroides maculatus

When puffers see danger coming, they puff up their bellies with air or water until they are almost as round as a ball, making it difficult for their predators to swallow them. These oval-shaped, chunky fishes have no scales or pelvic fins. Their teeth are fused together and form two platelike or beaklike teeth in each jaw.

Look for: A grayish-green puffer with blotches and small spots on back. Sides have irregular bars. Small spines or prickles on body except base of tail fin.

Length: 14".

HABITAT: Bays, estuaries, offshore to depths of 200'.

RANGE:

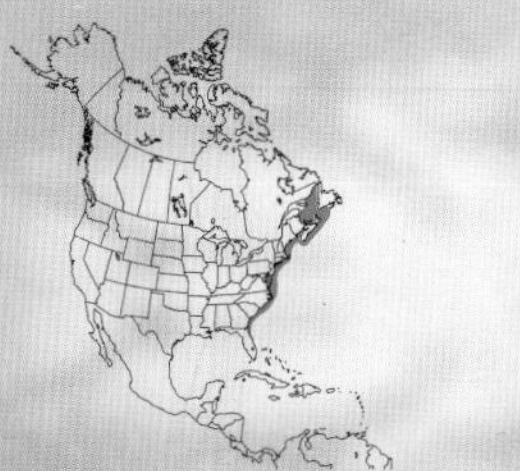

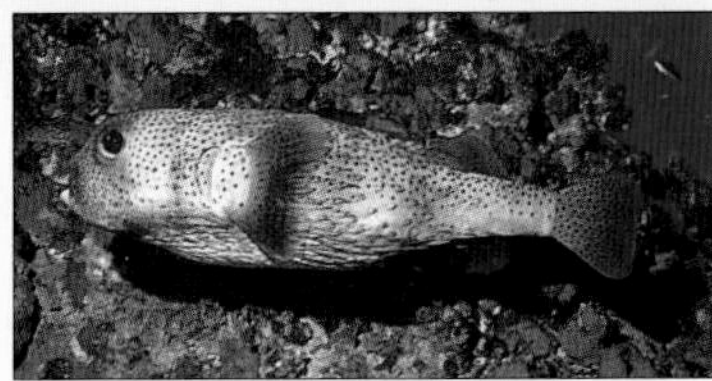

PORCUPINEFISH

Diodon hystrix

LOOK FOR: A large, gray pufferlike fish with black spots and long "porcupine" spines that fold when fish is not inflated. **LENGTH:** 24". **HABITAT:** Coral reefs and other shallow water habitats. **RANGE:** Massachusetts to Brazil, West Indies.

PACIFIC BURRFISH

Chilomycterus affinis

LOOK FOR: A fish with short, rigid spines. Bluish above and light below, dark spots on upper parts. **LENGTH:** 20". **HABITAT:** Shallow inshore waters. **RANGE:** Southern California to Galápagos Islands, Ecuador.

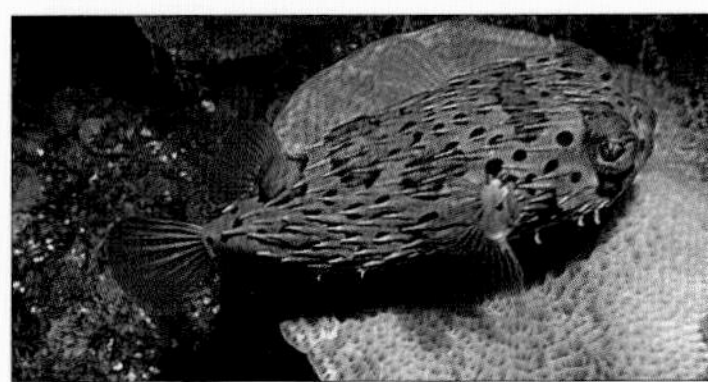

BALLOONFISH

Diodon holocanthus

LOOK FOR: A chunky, blunt-snouted fish covered in thick spines, longest on forehead. Light brown with dark spots. **LENGTH:** 18". **HABITAT:** Shallow coastal waters, coral reefs. **RANGE:** Gulf of California to Peru, Florida to Brazil, Gulf of Mexico.

Gray Angelfish page 129

How to use the reference section

The **Glossary,** which begins below, contains terms used by ichthyologists and naturalists. If you run across a word in this book that you do not understand, check the glossary for a definition. Also in this section is a listing of **Resources,** including books, videos, organizations, and Web sites devoted to North American fishes, as well as a table for learning how to convert measurements to metrics. Finally, there is an **Index** of all the species covered in the field guide section of this book.

GLOSSARY

Barbel
A whisker-like projection of skin, usually on the snout or chin.

Batoid
A type of fish with a flat disk-shaped body, such as a skate or ray.

Brackish
Describes a mixture of salt and fresh water.

Cartilaginous
Describes a skeleton made up of cartilage, a flexible material that supports the bones and organs inside a fish's body. Parts of the human body, like the nose and ears, also contain cartilage.

Compressed
Describes a fish body that is flattened on the sides.

Conical
Cone-shaped.

Depressed
Describes a fish body that is flattened top to bottom.

Dorsal
Describes something that is part of or on the back.

Drainage
An area where a river or stream flows into a larger body of water.

Elongate
Long and thin in shape, such as an eel.

Estuary
A passage where the fresh water of a river meets the salt water of an ocean or sea.

Fertilization
When a male animal's sperm is united with a female animal's egg. The fertilized egg then develops into a new animal.

Fresh water
A body of water that is not salty, like a river, pond, lake, or stream.

Juvenile
A young animal in the stage of growth between baby and adult.

Larva (plural: larvae)
A stage of growth before an animal reaches its mature form.

Mangrove
A type of tree that grows in groups on shorelines or in marshes.

Mottled
Describes something with blotches of different colors.

Nocturnal
Active at night.

Parasite
A creature which lives on or inside another creature and steals its nourishment.

Predator
An animal that hunts and kills other animals for food.

Prey
An animal caught by predators for food.

Scutes
Large, hardened scales.

Sea grass
A grass-like plant that grows in salty water.

Spawn
To release and fertilize eggs in the water.

Swim bladder
A gas-filled sac (like a small balloon) used by certain fishes to help them breathe and float in the water.

Territorial
Describes an animal that is protective of the area in which it lives.

Translucent
See-through, but not completely clear.

Tributary
A stream that runs into a larger body of water.

Tubercule
A small round-shaped lump or knot-like growth.

FOR FURTHER READING

Amazing Fish (Eyewitness Juniors)
Mary Ling and Jerry Young
Alfred A. Knopf, 1991

Stoplight Parrotfish page 135

Encyclopedia of Fishes
John R. Paxton, William N. Eschmeyer, and David Kirshner
Academic Press, 1998

Eyewitness Series: Fish
Steve Parker, Dave King, and Colin Keates
Alfred A. Knopf, 1990

The Fascinating Freshwater Fish Book: How to Catch, Keep, and Observe Your Own Native Fish
John R. Quinn
John Wiley & Sons, 1994

Fish (Our Living World)
Edward R. Ricciuti and William Simpson
Blackbirch Marketing, 1994

Fish Watching: An Outdoor Guide to Freshwater Fishes
C. Lavett Smith
Comstock Publishing Associates, 1994

Fishes: A Guide to Fresh & Salt Water Species (Golden Guides)
Herbert S. Zim, Hurst H. Shoemaker, and James G. Irving
Golden Books Publishing Company, 1987

How Fish Swim (Nature's Mysteries)
Jill Bailey
Benchmark Books, 1997

Informania Sharks
Christopher Maynard
Candlewick Press, 1997

National Audubon Society Field Guide to Fishes, Whales & Dolphins
Herbert T. Boschung, Jr., James D. Williams, Daniel W. Gotshall, David K. Caldwell, and Melba C. Caldwell
Alfred A. Knopf, 1983

National Audubon Society Field Guide to Tropical Marine Fishes
C. Lavett Smith
Alfred A. Knopf, 1997

Peterson First Guide to Fishes of North America
Michael Filisky and Roger Tory Peterson
Chapters Publishing, Ltd., 1998

Sharks & Rays (Nature Company Guide)
L. R. Taylor, Kevin Deacon, John E. McCosker, Peter R. Last, and Timothy C. Tricas
Time Life, 1997

They Swim the Seas: The Mystery of Animal Migration
Seymour Simon and Elsa Warnick
Browndeer, 1998

Tropical Reef Fishes
Gerald R. Allen, Roger Steene, and Rudie Kuiter
Charles E. Tuttle Company, 1997

What is a Fish?
Robert Snedden and Adrian Lascom
Sierra Club Juveniles, 1993

VIDEOS

Creatures of the Sea
NOVA Classroom Fieldtrips Series

Eyewitness Video: Fish
PBS Series, 1996

ORGANIZATIONS

Center for Marine Conservation
1725 DeSales Street NW
Suite 600
Washington, DC 20036
Tel: 202-429-5609
http://www.cmc-ocean.org

National Audubon Society
700 Broadway
New York, NY 10003-9562
Tel: 800-274-4201
http://www.audubon.org

National Fish and Wildlife Foundation
1120 Connecticut Avenue NW, Suite 900
Washington, DC 20036
Tel: 202-857-0166
http://www.nfwf.org

National Oceanic and Atmospheric Administration (NOAA)
1315 East-West Highway SSMC3
Silver Spring, MD 20910
http://www.nmfs.gov

The Nature Conservancy
International Headquarters
1815 North Lynn Street
Arlington, VA 22209
Tel: 703-841-5300
http://www.tnc.org

North American Native Fishes Association:
http://www.nanfa.org

U.S. Fish & Wildlife Service—National Fisheries Program
4401 North Fairfax Drive
MS810
Arlington, VA 22203
http://www.fws.gov/r9af

WEB SITES

Audubon's "Educate Yourself" Web site:
http://www.audubon.org/educate

FISH—A Quick Course on Ichthyology:
http://www.odysseyexpeditions.org/indexfish.htm

FishBase—A Global Information System on Fishes:
http://www.fishbase.org

National Museum of Natural History Fish Collection:
http://www.nmnh.si.edu/vert/fishcat/index.html

OceanLink:
http://www.oceanlink.island.net

U.S. Fish & Wildlife Service—Kid's Corner:
http://www.fws.gov/r9endspp/kid%5fcor/kid_cor.htm

World Wildlife Federation—Endangered Seas:
http://www.worldwildlife.org/yoto

Make it metric

Here is a chart you can use to change measurements of size, distance, weight, and temperature to their metric equivalents.

	multiply by
inches to millimeters	25
inches to centimeters	2.5
feet to meters	0.3
yards to meters	0.9
miles to kilometers	1.6
square miles to square kilometers	2.6
ounces to grams	28.3
pounds to kilograms	.45
Fahrenheit to Centigrade	subtract 32 and multiply by .55

INDEX

Page numbers in **bold type** point to a fish's page in the field guide.

Bluegill page 116

PHOTO CREDITS

Credits are listed by page, from left to right, top to bottom.

Front cover (Queen Angelfish): Charles V. Angelo/Photo Researchers, Inc.
Half-title page (Balloonfish): Renee DeMartin
Title page (Muskellenge): Bill Lindner Photography
Table of contents (French Grunts): Stephen Frink/Waterhouse

6: Doug Perrine/Innerspace Visions. **8a:** Ellan Young/Photo Researchers, Inc. **8b:** New York Aquarium. **9a:** Jessica Wecker/Photo Researchers, Inc. **9b:** Jessica Wecker/Photo Researchers, Inc. **9c:** Jessica Wecker/ Photo Researchers, Inc. **10–11:** Norbert Wu. **10a:** Bob Cranston. **11a:** James D. Watt/Innerspace Visions. **11b:** Michele R. Westmorland. **11c:** Harry M. Walker. **11d:** Alvin E. Staffan/Photo Researchers, Inc. **12a:** John G. Shedd Aquarium. **12b:** Gary Meszaros/Visuals Unlimited. **12c:** Patrice Ceisel/Visuals Unlimited. **13a:** Breck P. Kent. **13b:** Rob & Ann Simpson/Visuals Unlimited. **13c:** Norbert Wu. **14a** (Lemon Shark): Doug Perrine/Innerspace Visions. **14b:** Ken Lucas/Visuals Unlimited. **14c:** Clay H. Wiseman. **15a:** Breck P. Kent. **15b:** S. Maslowski/Visuals Unlimited. **15c:** J. Schauer/Aquatech. **16–17:** Bill Lindner Photography. **17a:** John Mitchell/Photo Researchers, Inc. **17b:** Stephen Frink/Waterhouse. **17c:** Timothy O' Keefe/Bruce Coleman, Inc. **18a:** Stephen Frink/Waterhouse. **18b** (Manta): Bob Cranston. **18c:** Aaron Ferster/Photo Researchers, Inc. **19a** (Sailfish): Avi Klapter/Mo Young Productions. **19b** (Spotted Trunkfish): Doug Perrine/Innerspace Visions. **19c:** Stephen Frink/Waterhouse. **20a:** Scot Stewart. **20b:** Phil Degginger/Color-Pic, Inc. **21a:** Herb Segars. **21b** (Great White Shark): James D. Watt/ Innerspace Visions. **21c:** John Morrissey/Innerspace Visions. **22–23:** Charles V. Angelo/Photo Researchers, Inc. **22a:** Mark Giovannetti/Prophoto. **23a:** James D. Watt/Waterhouse. **23b:** Roger Wilmshurst/Photo Researchers, Inc. **24a:** Rob & Ann Simpson. **24b:** Andrew J. Martinez. **24c:** Andrew G. Wood/Photo Researchers, Inc. **24d:** Larry Mishkar/PictureSmith. **25a:** David Hall/Photo Researchers, Inc. **25b:** Doug Stamm/Prophoto. **25c:** Norbert Wu. **26a:** Renee DeMartin. **26b:** Breck P. Kent. **26c:** Andrew Drake. **26d:** John G. Shedd Aquarium. **27a:** William H. Mullins/Photo Researchers, Inc. **27b:** Chris Huss. **28–29:** Wayne & Karen Brown/Brown & Company Photography. **28a:** Doug Perrine/ Innerspace Visions. **28b:** C. L. Smith/ Cornell University Press. **28c:** Garold W. Sneegas. **29a:** Jeffrey Rich. **29b:** Ted Clutter/Photo Researchers, Inc. **29c:** Bob DeGoursey/Visuals Unlimited. **30a:** James D. Watt/Mo Young Productions. **30b** (background): David Parker/SPL/Photo Researchers, Inc. **31a:** Doug Stamm/Prophoto. **31b** (background): Eda Rogers. **31c:** Hal Beral/Visuals Unlimited. **31d** (background): Steve Simonsen. **32a:** Herb Segars. **32b** (background): Rob & Ann Simpson. **32c:** Breck P. Kent. **32d** (background): Allen Blake Sheldon. **33a:** Dr. Charles Steinmetz, Jr. **33b** (background): Rob & Ann Simpson. **33c:** Bill Lindner Photography. **33d** (background): Jim Corwin/Photo Researchers, Inc. **34:** Mark Giovannetti/Prophoto. **35:** Stephen Frink/Waterhouse. **36a:** Jim Steinberg/Photo Researchers, Inc. **36b:** Fritz Polking/Visuals Unlimited. **37a:** Stephen Frink/Waterhouse. **37b:** Bill Buckley/The Green Agency. **37c:** Dale C. Spartas/The Green Agency. **38–39:** Andrew J. Martinez. **38a:** Doug Perrine/Innerspace Visions. **39a:** Mark Giovannetti/Prophoto. **39b:** David M. Schleser/Nature's Images. **39c:** Gary Meszaros/Visuals Unlimited. **40a:** Patrice Ceisel/John G. Shedd Aquarium. **40b:** Dr. Charles Steinmetz, Jr. **41a:** Andrew J. Martinez. **41b:** Wayne & Karen Brown/Brown & Company Photography. **41c:** James D. Watt/Mo Young Productions. **41d:** John G. Shedd Aquarium. **41e:** Gregory K. Scott/Photo Researchers, Inc. **41f:** Herb Segars. **41g:** Stuart Westmorland. **41h:** Tom McHugh/Steinhart Aquarium/Photo Researchers, Inc. **41i:** Dr. Charles Steinmetz, Jr. **42–43** (Yellow Perch): John G. Shedd Aquarium. **42a:** Susan E. Blanchet/Blanchet Photographics. **42b:** Wayne & Karen Brown/Brown & Company Photography. **43a:** Patrice Ceisel/Visuals Unlimited. **43b:** Scot Stewart. **43c:** Wayne & Karen Brown/Brown & Company Photography. **43d:** Wayne & Karen Brown/Brown & Company Photography. **43e:** Gary Meszaros/Visuals Unlimited. **43f:** Wayne & Karen Brown/Brown & Company Photography. **44–45:** Steven Frink/Waterhouse. **45a:** Charles V. Angelo/Photo Researchers, Inc. **45b:** Marty Snyderman/Waterhouse. **45c:** Robert J. Erwin/Photo Researchers, Inc. **46–47:** Bob Cranston. **46a:** Graeme Teague. **46b:** Breck P. Kent. **47a:** Ken Lucas/Visuals Unlimited. **47b:** Lance Beeny. **48:** Mark Giovannetti/Prophoto. **50:** Breck P. Kent. **51a:** Gary Meszaros/Visuals Unlimited. **51b** (inset): Breck P. Kent. **51c:** John G. Shedd Aquarium. **51d:** Brandon Cole/Mo Young Productions. **52:** Steve Simonsen. **53a:** Doug Perrine/Innerspace Visions. **53b:** Jeff Rotman/Innerspace Visions. **53c:** Chris Huss/Innerspace Visions. **54:** Edward G. Lines, Jr./John G. Shedd Aquarium. **55a:** Doug Perrine/ Innerspace Visions. **55b:** Herb Segars. **55c:** Joyce Burek. **56:** Rob & Ann Simpson. **57a:** John G. Shedd Aquarium. **57b:** John G. Shedd Aquarium. **58:** Patrice/Visuals Unlimited. **59a:** Patrice Ceisel/John G. Shedd Aquarium. **59b:** John G. Shedd Aquarium. **59c:** Gary Meszaros/ Visuals Unlimited. **60:** Stephen Frink/ Waterhouse. **61a:** John G. Shedd Aquarium. **61b:** Stephen Frink/ WaterHouse. **62:** Doug Stamm/ Prophoto. **63a:** Wayne & Karen Brown/Brown & Company Photography. **63b:** Stephen Frink/Water House. **64:** John G. Shedd Aquarium. **65a:** John G. Shedd Aquarium. **65b:** Thomas R. Lake. **65c:** David S. Addison/Visuals Unlimited. **66:** John G. Shedd Aquarium. **67a:** Alvin E. Staffan/Photo Researchers, Inc. **67b:** John G. Shedd Aquarium. **67c:** Glen M. Oliver/Visuals Unlimited. **68:** Breck P. Kent. **69a:** Gary Meszaros/ Bruce Coleman, Inc. **69b:** Alvin E.

Staffan/Photo Researchers, Inc. **69c:** James F. Parnell. **70:** Alvin E. Staffan/ Photo Researchers, Inc. **71a:** Edward G. Lines Jr./John G. Shedd Aquarium. **71b:** John G. Shedd Aquarium. **71c:** John G. Shedd Aquarium. **72:** Alvin E. Staffan/ Photo Researchers, Inc. **73a:** John G. Shedd Aquarium. **73b:** James F. Parnell. **73c:** John G. Shedd Aquarium. **74:** Gilbert Twiest/Visuals Unlimited. **75a:** John G. Shedd Aquarium. **75b:** Gary Meszaros/ Visuals Unlimited. **75c:** Rob & Ann Simpson. **76:** Patrice Ceisel/John G. Shedd Aquarium. **77a:** Edward G. Lines, Jr./John G. Shedd Aquarium **77b:** Ken Lucas/Visuals Unlimited. **78:** Breck P. Kent. **79a:** Mark Giovannetti/Prophoto. **79b:** Patrice Ceisel/John G. Shedd Aquarium. **79c:** John G. Shedd Aquarium. **80:** Mark Giovannetti/ Prophoto. **81a:** Mark Giovannetti/ Prophoto. **81b:** Herve Berthoule/ Jacana/Photo Researchers, Inc. **81c:** Ken Lucas/Visuals Unlimited. **82:** Mark Giovannetti/ Prophoto. **83a:** Tom Boyden. **83b:** Edward G. Lines Jr./John G. Shedd Aquarium. **83c:** Ken Lucas/Visuals Unlimited. **84:** Mark Giovannetti/ ProPhoto. **85a:** Bill Lindner Photography. **85b:** Tom McHugh/ Steinhardt Aquarium/Photo Researchers, Inc. **85c:** Gary Meszaros/Visuals Unlimited. **86:** John G. Shedd Aquarium. **87a:** Patrice Ceisel/Visuals Unlimited. **87b:** Joseph T. Collins/ Photo Researchers, Inc. **87c:** R. J. Goldstein/Visuals Unlimited. **88:** John G. Shedd Aquarium. **89a:** Andrew J. Martinez. **89b:** John G. Shedd Aquarium. **89c:** Donald Flescher. **90:** Herb Segars. **91a:** Jeff Mondragon. **91b:** Tom McHugh/ Steinhart Aquarium/Photo Researchers, Inc. **91c:** Mark Conlin. **92:** David B. Snyder. **93a:** Wayne & Karen Brown/ Brown & Company Photography. **93b:** Joyce Burek. **93c:** Steve Simonsen. **94:** Doc White/Innerspace Visions. **95a:** Norbert Wu. **95b:** John E. Randall. **95c:** Herb Segars. **96:** Eda Rogers. **97a:** Gary Meszaros/ Visuals Unlimited. **97b:** James F. Parnell. **97c:** Joe McDonald/Visuals Unlimited. **98:** Gary Meszaros/ Visuals Unlimited. **99a:** Patrice/ Visuals Unlimited. **99b:** David S. Addison/Visuals Unlimited. **99c:** Fred Rohde/Visuals Unlimited. **100:** Gary Meszaros/Visuals Unlimited. **101a:** Glen M. Oliver/Visuals Unlimited. **101b:** Patrice Ceisel/John G. Shedd Aquarium. **101c:** Gregory C. Jensen. **102:** E. R. Degginger/ Color-Pic, Inc. **103a:** Herb Segars. **103b:** Wayne & Karen Brown/Brown & Company Photography. **103c:** Doug Perrine/Innerspace Visions. **104:** Andrew J. Martinez. **105a:** Mark Giovannetti/Prophoto. **105b:** Gary Meszaros/Dembinsky Photo Associates. **105c:** Ken Lucas/Visuals Unlimited. **106:** Stephen Frink/ Waterhouse. **107a:** Dr. Charles Steinmetz, Jr. **107b:** Herb Segars. **107c:** Wayne & Karen Brown/Brown & Company Photography. **108:** Breck P. Kent. **109a:** Gary Meszaros/Visuals Unlimited. **109b:** John G. Shedd Aquarium. **109c:** Edward G. Lines Jr./John G. Shedd Aquarium. **110:** Breck P. Kent. **111a:** Alvin E. Staffan/Photo Researchers, Inc. **111b:** Scot Stewart. **111c:** J. R. Shute/Visuals Unlimited. **112:** Phil Degginger/Color-Pic, Inc. **113a:** Maslowski/Visuals Unlimited. **113b:** Patrice Ceisel/John G. Shedd Aquarium. **113c:** John G. Shedd Aquarium. **114:** E. R. Degginger/ Photo Researchers, Inc.**115a:** John G. Shedd Aquarium. **115b:** Rob & Ann Simpson. **115c:** Ken Lucas/Visuals Unlimited. **116:** James F. Parnell. **117a:** Rob & Ann Simpson/Visuals Unlimited. **117b:** Patrice Ceisel/John G. Shedd Aquarium. **117c:** David M. Schleser/Nature's Images. **118:** Dr. Charles Steinmetz, Jr. **119a:** John G. Shedd Aquarium. **119b:** David S. Addison/Visuals Unlimited. **119c:** Patrice Ceisel/John G. Shedd Aquarium. **120:** Wayne & Karen Brown/Brown & Company Photography. **121a:** Steve Simonsen. **121b:** Stephen Frink/WaterHouse. **121c:** Wayne & Karen Brown/Brown & Company Photography. **122:** Herb Segars. **123a:** Susan E. Blanchet/ Blanchet Photographics. **123b:** Fred McConnaughey/Photo Researchers, Inc. **123c:** Herb Segars. **124:** Mittelhaeuser Photography. **125a:** Steve Simonsen. **125b:** Michael Cardwell. **125c:** Stephen Frink/ Waterhouse. **126:** Tom McHugh/ Steinhart Aquarium/Photo Researchers, Inc. **127a:** Frank Burek. **127b:** Richard Herrmann. **127c:** Bob Cranston. **128:** Susan E. Blanchet/ Blanchet Photographics. **129a:** Susan E. Blanchet/Blanchet Photographics. **129b:** Steve Simonsen. **129c:** Fred McConnaughey/Photo Researchers, Inc. **130:** Andrew J. Martinez. **131a:** Joyce Burek. **131b:** Wayne & Karen Brown/Brown & Company Photography. **131c:** Robert E. Barber. **132:** Herb Segars. **133a:** Ken Lucas/Visuals Unlimited. **133b:** Patrice Ceisel/John G. Shedd Aquarium. **133c:** Steve Simonsen. **134:** David B. Snyder. **134a** (inset): Graeme Teague. **135a:** Fred McConnaughey/Photo Researchers, Inc. **135b:** Al Grotell. **135c:** Andrew J. Martinez. **136:** Graeme Teague. **137a:** David B. Snyder. **137b:** Steve Simonsen. **137c:** David B. Snyder. **138:** Stephen Frink/Waterhouse. **139a:** John G. Shedd Aquarium. **139b:** Fred Rohde/Visuals Unlimited. **139c:** Edward G. Lines Jr./John G. Shedd Aquarium. **140:** Doug Perrine/ Innerspace Visions. **141a:** Wayne & Karen Brown/Brown & Company Photography. **141b:** James D. Watt/Mo Young Productions. **141c:** George Lower/Photo Researchers, Inc. **142:** James F. Parnell. **143a:** Andrew J. Martinez. **143b:** Stephen Frink/Waterhouse. **143c:** Ken Lucas/Visuals Unlimited. **144:** John G. Shedd Aquarium. **145a:** Andrew J. Martinez/Photo Researchers, Inc. **145b:** Eda Rogers. **145c:** John G. Shedd Aquarium. **146:** Joyce Burek. **146a** (inset): Herb Segars. **147a:** David B. Snyder. **147b:** Doug Perrine/Innerspace. Visions. **147c:** Mittelhaeuser Photography. **148:** Ken Lucas/Visuals Unlimited. **149a:** Frank Burek. **149b:** Stephen Frink/ Waterhouse. **149c:** Graeme Teague. **150–151:** Steve Simonsen. **150a:** Susan Blanchet/Blanchet Photographics. **149c:** Stephen Frink/Waterhouse. **154:** Bill Lindner Photography.

Prepared and produced by
Chanticleer Press, Inc.

Publisher: Andrew Stewart
Founder: Paul Steiner

Chanticleer Staff:
Editor-in-Chief: Amy K. Hughes
Managing Editor: George Scott
Senior Editor: Miriam Harris
Associate Editor: Michelle Bredeson
Assistant Editor: Elizabeth Wright
Editorial Assistants: Amy Oh, Anne O'Connor
Photo Director: Zan Carter
Photo Editors: Ruth Jeyaveeran, Jennifer McClanaghan
Assistant Photo Editor: Meg Kuhta
Rights and Permissions Manager: Alyssa Sachar
Photo Assistants: Leslie Fink, Stephanie Wilson
Art Director: Drew Stevens
Designers: Anthony Liptak, Vincent Mejia, Bernadette Vibar
Director of Production: Alicia Mills
Production Manager: Philip Pfeifer
Production Assistant: Mee-So Caponi

Contributors:
Writer: C. Lavett Smith
Text Consultant: Rudolph Arndt
Icons: Vincent Mejia
Relief Map: Ortelius Design
Illustration: Howard S. Friedman

Scholastic Inc. Staff:
Editorial Director: Wendy Barish, Creative Director: David Saylor,
Managing Editor: Manuela Soares, Manufacturing Manager: Karen Fuchs

Original Series Design: Chic Simple Design